Praise for
The Executive Guide to High-Impact Talent Management

"There's no one-size-fits-all approach to talent management. This book gives leaders a practical guide for developing new workforce and leadership capabilities that can be adapted to any culture."
     —*Steve Goers, Vice President, Open Innovation, Kraft Foods*

"This book shows HR leaders how to create a more effective dialogue with their line executives to implement talent strategies that truly improve business performance."
     —*Dave Hemmer, President, Career Partners International*

"No executive is riding in on a white horse to solve critical talent issues today. Leaders must learn to collaborate with employees to create an environment that drives performance improvement. *The Executive Guide to High-Impact Talent Management* gives executives the essential tools needed to maximize the development of their future workforce."
     —*Van Wardlaw, Executive Vice President, Tennessee Valley Authority*

"This book gets past the human resources jargon that often numbs leaders into inaction. DeLong and Trautman give tools to both line executives and HR that show how to collaborate better to get real traction on critical talent problems."
     —*Larry Fagerhaug, Vice President of Organizational Development, Community Medical Center*

"Like most businesses, Aon Corporation must always look for ways to get better at developing tomorrow's leaders. With great examples from both large and small companies, DeLong and Trautman show how time-starved executives can have an immediate and lasting impact on their talent pipeline."
     —*Adam Stanley, Chief Technology Officer, Aon Corporation*

The

Executive Guide

to

HIGH-IMPACT
TALENT
MANAGEMENT

Powerful Tools for Leveraging
a Changing Workforce

DAVID DeLONG AND STEVE TRAUTMAN

New York Chicago San Francisco Lisbon London Madrid Mexico City
Milan New Delhi San Juan Seoul Singapore Sydney Toronto

The *McGraw·Hill* Companies

1 2 3 4 5 6 7 8 9 10 11 12 13 14 15 QFR/QFR 1 9 8 7 6 5 4 3 2 1 0

ISBN   978-0-07-173992-4
MHID   0-07-173992-0

This publication is designed to provide accurate and authoritative information in regard to the subject matter covered. It is sold with the understanding that neither the author nor the publisher is engaged in rendering legal, accounting, securities trading, or other professional services. If legal advice or other expert assistance is required, the services of a competent professional person should be sought.
—From a Declaration of Principles Jointly Adopted by a Committee of the American Bar Association and a Committee of Publishers and Associations

Library of Congress Cataloging-in-Publication Data

DeLong, David.
       The executive guide to high-impact talent management : powerful tools for leveraging a changing workforce / by David DeLong, Steve Trautman.
              p.   cm.
       Includes bibliographical references and index.
       ISBN 978-0-07-173992-4
       1. Manpower planning.   2. Personnel management.   3. Human capital—Management.   4. Executive ability.   I. Trautman, Steve.   II. Title.

       HF5549.5.M3D45   2011
       658.3—dc22   2010045505

McGraw-Hill books are available at special quantity discounts to use as premiums and sales promotions or for use in corporate training programs. To contact a representative, please e-mail us at bulksales@mcgraw-hill.com.

This book is printed on acid-free paper.

To our children, whose wisdom, kindness, and creative energy continually inspire us

DAVID: *For Anna and Sara*

STEVE: *For Grace and Lucas*

Contents

Acknowledgments

Every book is an adventure or an odyssey, depending on how you are feeling about the project that day. No effort like this could be completed without the direct and indirect support of hundreds of people who helped us along this journey. Over the past 20 years, our clients, workshop participants, and research partners have taught us a tremendous amount about the challenges of managing talent in the context of a changing workforce. Their courage to try innovative solutions—and to share their learning from those experiences—has been immensely helpful in shaping our thinking about what works and what doesn't.

We are particularly grateful to the more than 70 senior executives and talent management experts whom we interviewed as part of the research for this book. Thank you to Stephen Carlson, Sigrid Erdmann, Gary Kline, Laird Covey, Joe Wilczek, Jo Moore, Annmarie Neal, Hy Pomerance, Pauline Alten, Jim Paulson, Mike Short, and Mary Carvour, as well as many others who insisted on remaining anonymous. In addition, Lawrence Baxter, Larry Fagerhaug, and Van Wardlaw provided especially helpful feedback on early drafts. Riyad Qashu introduced us to an early version of the Knowledge Silo Matrix. Joe Coughlin, director of MIT's AgeLab, has continually been supportive of David's research, and Tom Davenport, Bettina Buechel, Preston Bottger, Andreas

Koenig, Brad Lawson, and Ellen Glanz were early partners on projects reported on here. Steve is also grateful to longtime collaborators and friends Sherryl Christie Bierschenk, Stacey Dickinson, and Todd Hudson.

Our book has also benefited from the patience and ever-enthusiastic support of our agent, Albert LaFarge. We owe a special thanks to McGraw-Hill acquisitions editor Judith McCarthy, who believed in our ideas from the beginning. The same encouragement has been repeatedly demonstrated by her colleagues Mary Glenn, Stephanie Frerich, Zach Gajewski, and Charlie Fisher.

We owe a special debt to our editor extraordinaire, Claire Greene, who was critical in shaping the manuscript and getting us to the finish line. In addition, David's intrepid research assistant Jennifer Munn was an incredibly diligent and productive partner in making this book a reality.

Acknowledgment is a totally inadequate word when it comes to thanking those closest to us for their support in seeing this project through. Plenty of people start writing books, but those who finish and stay sane in the process must have the encouragement of wonderful families. Both of us are incredibly blessed in that regard. David can't thank enough his unfailingly supportive wife, Sue Gladstone. His daughters, Sara and Anna, remained endlessly curious about the book's progress, particularly once they learned it was being dedicated to them. Steve's cheering section includes his wife, Sonja Gustafson, and his children, Lucas and Grace.

In the end, this book is a product of relationships. It has provided an opportunity to develop new connections, both personal and professional. Along the way, those relationships may turn out to be fleeting or lifelong. Either way, they have enriched our lives, and we are grateful for the chance to have learned from so many generous people.

Introduction

Organizations today need top executives who know how to lead strategic talent management efforts that maximize the performance of a dramatically changing workforce. No matter what you call the problems of recruiting, developing, and retaining great people, the challenges of talent management are well known throughout organizations today. Most executives recognize the importance of developing and sustaining a workforce and leadership team to support their strategy. They also know that the talent pool is changing. More and more baby boomers are retiring, and highly qualified midcareer leaders and technical talent are becoming harder to find. In addition, those new to the workforce definitely have different work styles and expectations about using technology on the job. If you're an executive, you've heard all this before.

You also have heard from your human resources (HR) department or your talent management staff about all the investments the organization has made—or needs to make— to support the development of your workforce. There are some pretty sophisticated "best practices" out there now that can make hiring more efficient, accelerate onboarding and leadership development, improve performance management, and increase retention of highly engaged employees. In fact, talent management programs and their related IT systems have become big business. So what's the problem?

The problem is, if you're a leader outside of HR, you most likely have a nagging feeling that your organization isn't getting its money's worth when it comes to talent management. Sure, the organization is spending a lot on its "people processes," but are those processes delivering what they're supposed to?

- Are your recruiting, performance management, and retention processes helping you achieve your short-term business objectives?
- Is your talent management strategy helping you build the workforce and leadership team you need to drive the business in the future?
- Do you even have a talent management strategy?
- Are you comfortable with the role you're playing in influencing it?
- Or is it better to just let HR run this talent business?

If you answered "no," "not sure," or "maybe" to any of these questions, this book is for you.

The problem, as our research and client work shows, is that executives have not been providing the leadership needed to build capabilities that will be required in the future. Leaders recognize the problems with talent management, but they are extremely frustrated when it comes to knowing what to do about them. This book answers the following questions:

- What is the *real* role of leaders (outside HR) in shaping and driving the organization's talent strategy?
- When it comes to talent management, how do you know you're doing your job well?

- Given limited time, how can executives maximize their impact in shaping the organization's talent processes?
- What specific actions can you take to collaborate more productively with your HR or talent management staff?

The Executive Guide to High-Impact Talent Management provides a logical framework and the practical tools leaders need to directly address these questions. This book helps readers translate their belief in the importance of investing in people into concrete actions that directly affect business performance.

Of course, the challenges of recruiting, developing, and retaining high-performing employees have always been important. But with massive changes coming in workforce demographics, the number of candidates in the age bracket that normally fills leadership roles will drop 30 percent by 2015, according to recent research. Assuming even moderate growth, this means many organizations will be left with about half the leadership talent they need.[1] Major corporations are also worried that the demands are so great today on senior executives working in fast-changing, complex, geographically distributed companies that fewer talented young managers are aspiring to senior leadership roles. Some evidence of this is found in the decreased mobility of high-potential candidates, who are less willing to move than in the past.

A shortage of leaders is only part of the problem. In knowledge-intensive sectors such as high technology, health care, aerospace and defense, energy, and even government, the development and retention of engineers, scientists, and other highly skilled professionals is an increasing challenge. Shortages of systems engineers, network architects, physicians, petroleum engineers, accountants, and risk managers all threaten the ability of organizations to compete and grow.

Thus, the role of leaders in managing talent has never been more critical. In the future, any executives serious about improving their organizations' performance must directly address the challenges of developing workforce and leadership capabilities if they are to avoid the unacceptable costs of major talent shortages. The question for most executives is, what do I do?

This book is based on the premise that the primary reason leaders are not more effective in directing or collaborating with HR on these issues is that they simply don't know where to begin—given all the other demands on their time. This book changes the game. It is written with a proactive orientation for top managers who want to know what practical steps they can take immediately to improve the impact of talent management practices, programs, and processes. *The Executive Guide to High-Impact Talent Management* helps leaders balance strategic and tactical considerations about the talent-related risks facing their organization. Readers in other roles, however, will also find help here.

Human resource and talent management professionals will find a section at the end of each chapter with suggestions and questions they can use to adapt the tools and frameworks in their own work. It will also show how HR professionals can most effectively share the book's ideas with line executives. For example, if line leaders aren't pushing an in-depth conversation about the strategic context that should drive talent initiatives, a section at the end of Chapter 3 shows how to begin engaging executives in that discussion.

Middle managers will discover skills they need to improve their own competencies and reputation in managing talent.

Tools like the Knowledge Silo Matrix and the "Big Picture" strategy questions can be used immediately with departments and teams to improve onboarding, skill development, and the quality of decision making.

Consultants and vendors will find the book gives them a language and framework to talk with potential executive sponsors by breaking free of burdensome HR jargon that often puts leaders on the defensive. For example, Chapters 4 and 8 will help suppliers show line executives how they can help mitigate talent-related risks that clearly threaten business performance.

Management professors and leadership trainers can use this book as a valuable supplement in leadership courses, where it can be used to educate new managers about competencies they will need to advance their careers. In the years ahead, virtually every manager will be judged on his or her ability to manage talent. It will become a core competency, and this book can serve as a resource in developing those skills.

The Executive Guide to High-Impact Talent Management is organized into three sections. Chapters 1 through 4 will help you clarify the talent problem in your organization from a leadership perspective. Chapter 1 provides a checklist of the most costly talent issues that executives fail to address. Problems such as a dangerously thin leadership pipeline, failure to develop capabilities needed to drive a new strategy, and poor productivity of new hires are explored. Chapter 2 offers an executive framework for talent management, highlighting the activities where leaders can have the greatest impact in shaping future workforce capabilities. This model is a core part of the book and can serve as a checklist during future initiatives. Chapters 3 and 4 provide powerful tools for diagnosing talent-related risks and for aligning business strategy and talent processes. These tools have demonstrated their value in many organizations and industries.

The middle of the book focuses on evaluating initiatives and innovative solutions to talent management challenges. Chapter 5 provides practical approaches for evaluating the performance of existing investments, whether a full-blown inventory or the assessment of a specific program. Perhaps more important, Chapter 5 shows how organizational culture often determines the success of talent initiatives. It includes a useful diagnostic that executives can use to communicate cultural principles that should drive their company's recruiting, development, and retention programs. For example, some firms are committed to promoting leaders from within, and thus need to make sure all initiatives are aligned to support this cultural norm.

Dramatic changes are coming in the global talent pool, and a great number of companies are already aware of the threats they face. Thus, it is surprising how many organizations continue to pursue relatively routine, "me-too" talent management solutions. Chapters 6 and 7 describe some of the most innovative solutions we've found in our research and work with clients. What defines success in all cases here is the clear impact on business performance. It may be Microsoft's use of an internship program that directly improves its long-term *quality of hires.* Or maybe you can learn from a North Carolina hospital whose program to reenergize high-performing nurses has a 97 percent retention rate, essential for supporting hospital growth. With more than one-third of new senior executives failing in their new roles within 18 months, the cost to organizations of unsuccessful transitions is enormous. Chapter 7 also includes the story of a customized program, first developed in Pfizer Pharmaceuticals, that has proved highly effective at increasing the success rate of executive transitions. The solutions described in these two chapters won't make you an expert in talent management, but they can help you better understand your own challenges and analyze the solutions presented to you.

The book's last three chapters are loaded with ideas and frameworks to clarify the executive's role in implementing talent initiatives. Ultimately, to improve recruiting, performance management, leadership development, and employee retention, leaders need to change the behaviors and decisions made on a daily basis in their organizations. Driving this change first requires effective measurement systems. Chapter 8 shows how to cut through the tidal wave of HR metrics that threaten to overwhelm any leader trying to make a difference. This chapter contains the key questions executives must ask to get the relevant information they need that will ensure talent investments are contributing to business outcomes.

Chapter 9 provides action steps for the executive's three most critical tasks in implementing talent initiatives: clarifying sponsorship roles and activities, creating and sustaining urgency around a project, and driving more integrated solutions. This chapter outlines the questions leaders need to ask their HR staff to make sure the organization's larger needs for integration of talent management processes are being addressed. Finally, Chapter 10 reports on six lessons from our most recent research that show current talent-related issues in which executives can have an immediate impact.

This book's ambitious goal is to provide an executive perspective on talent management that is relevant across sectors, business units, and functions. The highly contextual nature of talent and the wide range of variables involved make narrow quantitative studies irrelevant to executive decision makers. Rather, we share nuanced insights based on our intensive experience working with clients and on interviews with more than 70 senior executives and talent management experts in dozens of organizations around the world.

The Executive Guide to High-Impact Talent Management is a practical book, but it's not a cookbook. You won't find any formulas or recipes here. That's because every organization's strategy, culture, competitive environment, and geographic location dictates a different talent management strategy. Where and how you focus your efforts will depend on your role in the organization and the state of your existing talent management infrastructure. There are no simple solutions, but we will give you lots of ideas on what works and how to have an impact fast.

In the past decade, many excellent books have described different aspects of the changing workforce.[2] This book is not one of them. Nor is *The Executive Guide to High-Impact Talent Management* another book that aims to serve a general HR audience. There have been plenty of those, some excellent.[3] But they don't speak to the needs of the senior line executive. This book is for leaders.

As a leader, you face countless requests for your time and your support. Ultimately, your success depends on your ability to relentlessly focus your organization on the few priorities that are critical to success. If your intent is to manage talent more effectively, this book will provide the frameworks and tools you need to take effective action—starting today.

1

The New Role for Leaders
in Managing Talent

Every organization where skilled employees are a key source of competitive advantage needs senior executives (outside the HR department) who know how to *lead* strategic talent management initiatives. But when it comes to recruiting, developing, and retaining top talent, there is a disconnect between what executives say and what executives do. Research studies consistently show that senior managers have become very concerned about talent management and leadership development in the last decade. Top executives worldwide ranked human capital risks as the most serious challenge facing their global operations, according to a study by the *Economist* Intelligence Unit.[1] More than 90 percent of organizations reported their senior leaders believe that outstanding talent is essential to competitive advantage, said Hewitt Associates. Leadership's growing interest in the importance of talent management has been confirmed repeatedly in other studies.[2]

But leaders, while deeply concerned about managing talent, can find it difficult to approach these challenges with the sort of focus, discipline, and action they would apply to problems in finance, supply chain management, manufacturing, marketing, and customer service. This book will help executives bring that kind of rigor to talent management. It answers the question, What is the senior manager's *real job* in developing future workforce and leadership capabilities at this critical time in history?

Executive Responses to Talent-Related Risks: Alarm, Overconfidence, Denial

The following three examples show how top managers' responses to talent management challenges range from alarm to overconfidence to denial. Our stories come from the high-tech, consumer products, and health-care industries, and they show that these problems affect organizations of all sizes.

Alarm: "How Are We Going to Get the People We Need to Grow This Business?"

When he looked at his small staff and leadership team, the new COO for a $20 million software company wasn't sure he could meet the owner's aggressive revenue targets. This firm, which is a leading supplier of software for the commercial construction industry, had recently secured an infusion of capital to support growth opportunities. Now the COO had to deliver on his boss's promise. But this meant expanding the sales force from 3 to 20 reps, in part because of plans to enter markets in two other countries. The owner also expected a high level of customer service to be maintained, which meant the professional services and customer support teams would need to expand by 50–80 percent in the next year. This rate of growth would be difficult under any circumstances, but the firm didn't have the talent management processes and practices in place to make it happen. Without these capabilities, the COO knew his team would struggle to balance hiring sufficient staff without bringing them on too soon. At the same time, he worried about creating a pipeline of leadership talent that could support future growth. He also wanted to maximize the productivity of new hires. How would this all get done, he wondered.

One of the most common scenarios we find is leaders who are concerned either because they lack the necessary talent management infrastructure to support business growth or because their talent processes are suddenly proving to be inadequate when confronted with major changes in work-force demographics. In both cases, senior executives worry about limitations imposed by a shortage of skilled talent, but they're unsure what to do about it.

Overconfidence: "What's Going on Here? I Thought We Had Talent Management Handled."

Here's another common scenario. Since taking over as head of a $17 billion United Kingdom–based consumer products company, the new CEO had committed to turning his company's decentralized multinational business into an integrated global enterprise. To implement this new strategy, the firm needed a robust pipeline of leadership talent. This shouldn't have been a problem because improving talent management in the company had been a priority for almost a decade. Innovations included the introduction of a process to identify high-potential candidates, an accelerated management training program, and annual succession planning throughout the firm.

"As a company, we had everything in place. It was text-book talent management," recalled one senior manager. The firm's HR department also continually benchmarked its talent processes against other leading organizations. These exercises convinced management that they were close to "best practice."

But when the HR director decided to conduct a detailed analysis of the succession pipeline, the chief executive gained some alarming insights. Despite what appeared to be a strong talent management program, the company was facing a serious shortage of qualified successors ready to fill the firm's top 200 senior positions. Out of 2,900 middle managers, only 15 percent were judged as high potentials. The corporation's management training program clearly was not producing enough qualified candidates for top jobs. In addition, about 75 percent of senior managers were staying in their current jobs less than two years, which meant leaders did not have time to develop their successors, nor was good succession planning a criterion for promotion.

Despite large investments in talent management initiatives, the CEO realized that the current state of the firm's talent pool represented an unacceptable risk that threatened his aggressive growth strategy. He was especially concerned because there were no plans in place to fix the growing shortage of talent needed to create an integrated global enterprise.

Many executives are leading organizations like this today. They know talent management is critical to long-term performance. They're investing millions to develop future workforce and leadership capabilities, and they can point to all kinds of "best practice" initiatives. But, when challenged, can they really be confident they have a qualified pool of successors, just because the firm has a program called "succession planning"?

Denial: "Talent Management? I Don't Have Time for That!"

Still other senior managers believe they don't need to worry about or can't afford to invest in talent management or leadership development initiatives. For example, as the last recession was winding down, the CEO of a regional hospital said,

> *Someone stopped me the other day in town and asked how things were going. I told him, "Except for a pending flu pandemic, the worst recession in history, the current debate on health-care reform, and the state just cut our Medicaid reimbursement, things are fine." I mean how many crises can you deal with at once?*

This executive insisted that workforce issues were no longer a primary concern for him because baby boomer retirements had slowed and there now seemed to be plenty of skilled health-care professionals available.

Whether they admit it publicly or not, plenty of executives today—like this hospital CEO—feel bombarded by a wide range of strategic issues. As a result, they see talent management, leadership development, and strategic workforce planning as strictly HR issues not needing their time and attention. These leaders often find subordinates' requests for support and resources bothersome and unnecessary.

These three scenarios in a growing high-tech firm, a global consumer products company, and a regional hospital characterize typical responses of senior executives when they are faced with talent management or strategic workforce planning issues. Many leaders, like the software company COO, suddenly realize they lack the talent management infrastructure needed to support continued growth. Other executives, like the consumer products CEO, are actively involved in overseeing investments in talent management and leadership development, but they aren't getting the expected results. And many senior managers still assume talent management decisions should be delegated to the HR department, which greatly increases the risk that these programs won't be aligned to support business strategy.

Talent: Can It Get Any More Complicated Than This?

No generation of executives has faced such a complex and difficult set of workforce challenges that today include:

- Increasingly dispersed employees are working across cultures, time zones, and reporting structures. In most organizations, greater cultural diversity, increased geographic distribution of operations, and more decentralized management structures have become a way of life.
- Regular churn of employees has become the norm, despite the temporary respite created by the last recession. Employees hired today can't be expected to stay as long as those hired 20 years ago.
- There are growing shortages of skills in critical roles, such as nurse managers, systems engineers, geoscientists, and experienced project managers, due primarily to the retirement of aging baby boomers.
- Another segment of aging workers, paradoxically, are staying on the job longer than expected because of inadequate retirement savings. These employees must be kept productive, and their extended tenure is slowing career advancement for restless midcareer employees.

- Most organizations face a dearth of leadership talent in the middle ranks, a by-product of years of downsizing and limited hiring, combined with the smaller size of Generation X. As a result, the competition for highly skilled midcareer employees is becoming more intense.
- Mergers and acquisitions, reorganizations, and out-sourcing demand much greater flexibility to "inhale and exhale" workers from any given project at any given moment. Global competition, frequent restructuring, and rapidly changing skill needs mean organizations can be laying off and hiring employees at the same time.
- Complex operational and strategic knowledge critical to performance is increasingly at risk due to layoffs, retirements, and reorganizations. The loss of unique experiential knowledge in areas such as R&D, sales, maintenance, and systems integration can have a direct impact on an organization's ability to grow, innovate, and maintain efficient, low-cost operations.[3]
- Four generations with distinctly different orientations to work, technology, communication, and learning are leading to increased conflict in the workplace. There is a compelling need to integrate Millennials, Gen Xers, baby boomers, and Traditionals in more collaborative work environments.

How Talent Management Failures Hurt Business Performance

Given these widely recognized workforce challenges, it's not surprising that surveys consistently report executives are uncertain about how to best source, develop, and retain the talent they need to beat the competition and grow the business.[4] If you're like most leaders coping with these changes, you've had limited success getting your talent management initiatives to directly support your business strategy. According to one study, less than 20 percent of organizations are consistently aligning and integrating talent initiatives with their overall business goals.[5] In practice, these disconnects have a variety of negative impacts. We have identified three types of common business problems caused by inadequate talent management. They can be characterized as: (1) succession planning challenges; (2) failure to fill emerging capability gaps; and (3) inadequate career development and training. See if these problems sound familiar.

Succession Planning Challenges

Here are three examples where failing to anticipate and make hard decisions about future leadership capabilities can have a direct impact on business performance.

"There's No One in the Wings to Replace Our Departing Executives"

In 2010, Genzyme CEO Henri Termeer found himself locked in a nasty proxy fight with activist shareholder Carl Icahn, in part, because the founder of this once high-flying biotechnology firm had refused to plan for his own succession. An analyst closely following Genzyme said Termeer's refusal to identify a successor after 25 years as CEO definitely contributed to uncertainty among investors and incited activist shareholders who wanted to sell the company.

One of the worst examples of failed succession planning is found in the tangled demise of Merrill Lynch, where chairman and CEO Stanley O'Neal presided over a company that in 2007 and 2008 lost more than $50 billion in shareholder value. While keeping his board of directors in the dark about the company's overinvestment in toxic subprime mortgage bonds, the CEO also eliminated any credible successors for his job. Thus, when the board finally forced O'Neal to "retire" in October 2008, it had to conduct a desperate search for a new leader because no succession planning had been done.[6]

It's hard to overestimate the costs of these colossal failures in succession planning. Yet the trend continues. A recent study by Stanford University and search firm Heidrick and Struggles found 51 percent of firms surveyed could not name a CEO successor if their chief executive was suddenly unavailable.[7] In addition, almost 40 percent of companies studied reported having no viable internal candidates for the job. These facts ignore the negative impact on the reputation of a firm and its brand and the lost productivity among senior staff caused by the uncertainty of succession. These outcomes combined with the negative impact on morale and productivity of frontline employees cost organizations millions of dollars.

Of course, some leaders understand this risk. Compare the behavior of Termeer and O'Neal with their counterpart at JP Morgan. In 2009, CEO Jamie Dimon identified his own successor, even though he was only 53 and had no intention of leaving the bank. Dimon explained, "It's my duty to the board to focus on succession. It's important that we have people trained and tested with experience to succeed me."[8] Turnover in senior executive ranks will continue to accelerate in the next decade as more baby boomer leaders retire, and the competition for top talent will become more frenzied. Thus, failing to prepare viable and committed candidates for succession will be much more costly to the organization.[9]

"We Don't Have Anyone to Run the New Unit"

"When we expanded the business last year, we realized we didn't have anyone to run the new division. In fact, our leadership pipeline is pretty thin." Of course, the needs for succession planning below the top management team are hard to predict and vary by organization. It's always possible an organization will end up investing in too many potential young leaders, although in the current environment it's more likely firms won't develop enough talent.[10] Having too many potential leaders means wasted resources and frustrated staff who lack opportunities. But having too few potential leaders—a much more common scenario today—limits the potential for growth and innovation. Many companies fail to even define the leadership traits they value most, much less try to develop these in their young managers.

A shortage of inside talent means recruiting and hiring leaders from outside the organization. How practical is this, given your industry, specific skill needs, and the geographic location of the positions you need to fill? What are the costs of investing in too many leadership candidates versus not having enough? Consider the growing number of organizations that have had to limit growth because they couldn't find the leadership talent needed to run new operations. One pharmaceutical company, for example, couldn't pursue new opportunities in the marketplace because it had no one in the organization with the talent needed to commercialize its products in promising new ways, and these leadership skills were not readily available in the marketplace.

As a senior executive, if you don't engage your subordinates on hard questions about the organization's *real* bench strength, you're greatly increasing the risk that your firm's leadership pipeline won't be calibrated to meet the company's future needs.

"How Do We Decide Whom to Invest In?"

"Employees don't plan to stay with our company for a lifetime, so how do we decide whom to invest in?" As more baby boomers retire, many organizations are feeling pressure to accelerate the development of their younger professionals and middle managers. We hear this refrain repeatedly in organizations today: "We only have a few years to get our high potentials 20 years of experience." But given the high rates of attrition when the job market is strong, there is lots of uncertainty about which employees are worth investing in. Who will stay, and who will leave? What is the best way to accelerate employees' development? Rotational assignments, special projects, and so on? How much potential does a specific individual really have? Is it more cost effective to wait and buy this resource on the market in a few years? How can we weed out poor performers early?

Predicting the outcomes of accelerating employee development can be highly uncertain, but avoiding investments to create a succession pipeline is not usually the solution. You need to decrease the likelihood that key high potentials will bolt when new opportunities arise, and learn how to maximize investments in all employees, no matter how long they stay. Otherwise, you can't reduce the risk of not having a ready workforce and leadership pipeline.

Failure to Fill Emerging Capability Gaps

Here are three common scenarios that reflect inadequate top management attention paid to the workforce and leadership skills needed to succeed in a changing competitive environment.

"We're Not Developing the Capabilities We'll Need to Implement Our New Strategic Plan"

In recent years, Canada Post's (CP) volume of mail delivered to residential homes dropped significantly as customers increasingly turned to electronic communication. In the same period, competitors roared to life challenging the lucrative express mail business. CP had an enviable distribution system and experienced workforce but needed a new strategy. Canada Post needed to rethink its direction and retool its operation or risk major financial losses.

As senior leaders set a new strategy, the next question was, Who will do the work? The new business direction wasn't just about efficiently sorting and delivering basic mail. It would require technical and logistical skills of a different sort, and there was no guarantee that existing staff could get the job done.[11]

It's always hard to predict whether or not a new strategy will be successful—especially if there is any uncertainty about the workforce. Like CP, organizations implementing a new strategy can't afford not to have essential new skills and capabilities in place. But it's surprising how often these risks and potential costs are not clearly understood. Most executives will focus on whether they've budgeted enough headcount to get a job done, but they avoid knowing whether they have the *right* headcount. That level of detail is usually deemed a lower-level manager's problem. But, you must be able to assess the real readiness to deliver on changing objectives, or your new business strategy is much more likely to fail.

"We're Not Sure We Should Keep Investing in Our New Operations"

A few years ago a major high-tech firm rapidly set up operations in India, primarily because its competitors had already done so. The immediate objective was to reduce the engineering costs of maintaining its mature products, which could be serviced by cheaper labor overseas. In addition, the company wanted to expand its corporate presence into major developing countries. So product managers were simply told to move a certain percentage of their workforce to India within the next year. Leaders paid no attention to which specific capabilities should be moved or what the practical effects would be of these shifts.

To date, this firm has invested more than $500 million building new offices in India and has several thousand full-time employees in the country. But trade-offs between reduced labor costs and diminished productivity of a less experienced workforce mean top management is still trying to figure out whether the investment was worth it. In addition, company leaders are now unsure what capabilities they should be developing in their Indian staff to support future business objectives. They also need new capabilities in their U.S. managers who are being called on to oversee foreign operations.

Organizations have invested billions of dollars in offshoring and outsourcing deals over the last decade. Some have clearly produced a great ROI, but many others have generated much more uncertain results. Leaders are left wondering if they should continue these investments in new sources of capabilities, expand them, or cut their losses and run. Each alternative presents its own set of uncertainties.

Executives must be able to evaluate the costs of different solutions for sourcing capabilities, or they are likely to take on new outsourcing risks whose cost/benefit trade-offs are out of balance. As a result, firms are much more likely to make bad talent management bets.

"Our Backlog and Contractor Costs Are Growing, and We're Having Quality Problems"

The oil spill in the Gulf of Mexico in 2010 was only one of a series of recent calamities for energy giant BP where the lack of capabilities had disastrous consequences. In early 2006, more than 200,000 gallons of crude oil spilled onto Alaska's North Slope, forcing BP to shut down the largest U.S. oil field. This meant 8 percent of U.S. domestic oil production was suddenly unavailable because of extensive corrosion in BP's oil pipelines. Before that series of leaks was discovered, the job of BP's senior corrosion engineer had gone unfilled for more than a year, which meant the firm no longer had an adequate strategic overview of its corrosion prevention activities.

It may seem difficult to predict what particular skills, capabilities, and knowledge might be hurt by turnover—and when. But it's straightforward to identify all critical silos of knowledge and determine costs to your business if those capabilities are seriously compromised. BP's leaders failed to understand the risks posed by losing corrosion expertise. And, although it looks small compared to the costs of the Gulf spill cleanup, failing to manage this knowledge base cost the energy giant millions of dollars.

Not only did BP sustain extensive losses in revenues as a result of the Alaska spill, it also faced embarrassing congressional hearings where leaders had to admit that BP had failed to meet its obligations to customers and the public. In addition, the company was forced to invest unexpectedly in rebuilding its corrosion prevention capabilities, hiring expensive outside experts to evaluate existing capabilities, and improving its corrosion prevention policies.[12] This scenario will probably repeat itself over and over again in the years ahead, although on a much less public stage. Organizations are likely to see complex technical, production, and delivery systems disrupted as more veteran experts retire, taking with them unique knowledge needed to diagnose and fix problems.

You must be clear about what specific capabilities or areas of expertise are critical to your business—and hard to replace. Otherwise, you increase the risk of developing costly knowledge shortages in essential areas.

Inadequate Career Development and Training

Finally, we've found two costly problems that reflect inadequate attention from leaders on how to maximize the productivity of junior staff and new hires.

"We're Not Getting High-Level Productivity Out of Our Next Generation of Talent"

A mechanical engineering firm with about 350 employees had hired only a handful of new engineers over the last 10 years. These "kids" were distributed around the organization, placed in teams that had been stable and working together in some cases for decades. The onboarding experience of the new engineers was inconsistent at best. Some of them were expected to "shadow" one senior engineer on a complex task for a month or two before being passed on to the next. The rotation was intended to give a broad background without expecting the new engineer to actually take on any responsibility. This sounded good until you talked with the engineers in the rotation. They described it as "years of wandering from team to team, always observing but never *doing* anything, with no end in sight." Other new engineers were given very discrete tasks such as document review or calculations in one unique area of work. The assumption was that once they were good at something, it was best to leave them where they could be useful "and not get underfoot."

Excessive use of job rotations, assigning tasks that are too narrow, or simply ignoring new hires is symptomatic of a firm with no clear strategy for developing and retaining its young talent. The result is unpredictable turnover and inconsistent productivity. This undisciplined approach also increases the risk of developing a bad reputation among a young, wired population who readily share opinions among classmates and potential recruits in a tightening labor market.

If your career development and training programs are uncoordinated and insensitive to the interests of younger employees, you run a much greater risk of increased attrition and having a workforce unprepared for the future.

"It Takes Our New Employees Too Long to Get Up to Speed"

A large mining company in the southwestern United States was facing a challenge common to many industrial operations: booming demand for its product required many new hires. This required the rapid onboarding of new employees, many of them into highly dangerous jobs.

As a result, the mine was experiencing considerably more recordable safety incidents and lost-time accidents among employees who had been on the job less than 120 days, and the productivity of the newest hires was well below expectations. It also had a very high rate of attrition among new hires because the new employees would get scared or hurt, or they would find the working conditions too difficult to manage on their own and quit. The challenge was how to keep new workers safe, get them up to full production quickly, and help them feel connected to their crews, while also stemming the new hire attrition rate.

It may be hard to predict how many new hires will actually stay with your firm and how successful they will be. But it's not as difficult to estimate the costs of failing to retain a high percentage of new employees or of failing to get them productive quickly. You should insist that your subordinates determine the costs of errors, productivity variances, and attrition. Otherwise, you are less likely to invest in new "onboarding" training solutions that will improve retention and productivity of new hires. This increases the likelihood that turnover costs will increase and productivity will not improve.

To Improve Talent Management, Lead from a Strategic—Not HR—Perspective

Do you see yourself or your organization confronting any of the problems we've just described? What are the responses your human resources or talent management team have suggested to address these threats to performance? Let us guess. They have sought to implement new systems, processes, or programs, such as those listed in Table 1.1.

There is nothing inherently wrong with these solutions. In fact, quite the opposite. Each can have a critical role in talent and leadership development. *But how much confidence do you have that your HR or talent management team understands how these investments are going to help you implement your business strategy?* Do they directly address the pain described in the scenarios in the preceding section? Executives in organizations where skilled employees are a key

TABLE 1.1   Common Talent Management Initiatives

Strategic workforce planning	High potential talent pools
Succession planning	Mentoring
Career development	Talent reviews
Management development or training	Web 2.0 or social media applications
Building an engagement culture	Phased retirement
Leadership development	Talent management IT systems
Accelerated onboarding	Lessons learned databases
Recruiting	Internships
Collaborative partnerships with outsourcing vendors	Performance management

asset can lead strategic talent management efforts by being better "customers" to those who are doing the work, as we will explain throughout the book.

Unfortunately, our research and client work show that top managers confronted with these workforce challenges often fail to provide the leadership needed. Two barriers in particular make it difficult for executives to effectively oversee talent management strategies: confusing language and lack of clarity about the executive's real role.

Make Language Work for Your Organization

A raft of excellent books written primarily for an HR audience describe what organizations should do to manage talent effectively. Some of the best business researchers in the world have applied themselves to these issues.[13] Their books are full of new strategies, frameworks, and principles for developing the capabilities of your workforce. But their detailed descriptions of strategic workforce planning processes, human capital strategies, talent management systems, and other HR buzzwords move the focus from strategic goals to minutia.

Their language does not have to be your language. Talent management concepts are highly abstract and potentially ambiguous, making miscommunication a routine challenge and progress very hard to measure. (See how to clarify the jargon in the sidebar "Talent Management Terminology: How It All Fits Together" on pages 20–22.) Therefore, you as a leader need to establish a clear shared understanding among the key stakeholders in your firm about your objectives. When terms like "global human capital strategy" or "lessons learned database" or "management training" start flying, don't just smile and nod. Stop the conversation and say, "I want to make sure we're all in agreement on what these terms mean. Here's what I think they mean." The overlapping concepts in Figure 1.1 show why there is often confusion about "people strategies."

FIGURE 1.1   Reduce Conceptual Confusion About Human Capital, Strategic Workforce Planning, and Talent Management

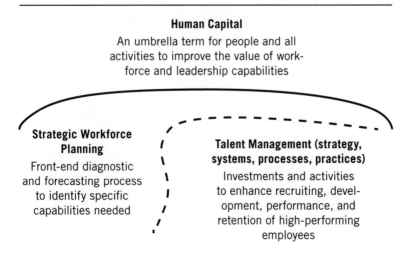

Human Capital
An umbrella term for people and all activities to improve the value of workforce and leadership capabilities

Strategic Workforce Planning
Front-end diagnostic and forecasting process to identify specific capabilities needed

Talent Management (strategy, systems, processes, practices)
Investments and activities to enhance recruiting, development, performance, and retention of high-performing employees

Talent Management Terminology: How It All Fits Together

Three terms are commonly used when talking about improving workforce and leadership capabilities. In practice, these concepts often mean different things from one organization to another. All that matters is that you agree within your organization what you are trying to change. Here is the way these terms are most commonly used today.

Human capital is the broadest term and is often used interchangeably to mean "people" and "human resources." Although it was first developed as an economic concept in the 1960s,[14] it is generally used today in the context of "human capital strategy" or "planning." One problem with *human capital* is that it can mean both individual and organizational capabilities. Are you focused on improving "the aggregate knowledge, skills, abilities, and other competencies" of your workforce?[15] Or are you talking about an individual's general or specific skills?

Workforce planning historically has described an operational process run by human resources to project short-term headcount. But "strategic workforce planning" has become a more fashionable term to describe a "forecasting and planning process that connects and directs talent management activities."[16] It usually refers to the *front-end* data collection, analysis, and forecasting activities that help executives understand what kinds of skills and capabilities they will need in the next two to five years.

Like human capital, strategic workforce planning can be used to describe activities at different levels. In its most strategic use, workforce planning refers to an analysis of the staffing implications for alternative business strategies. For example, how will our staffing needs differ if we grow by acquisition or launch a new business? Strategic workforce planning is also used to model the effects of more tactical human resource programs, such as outsourcing a particular unit or developing staff internally. To further confuse things, the term is sometimes used to describe the analysis of individual roles or the characteristics of employees (e.g., an age profile) and the implications for business performance. If you use the term *workforce planning*, be clear about the type of analysis you are looking for.

Talent management can describe all manner of efforts to improve workforce and leadership capabilities.[17] It typically refers to investments or activities that include recruitment, hiring, development, and retention of employees. It may refer to all of these stages in the employment life cycle, or just one particular area, such as leadership development or performance management. Talent management is applied to strategies, processes, systems, or projects. It's up to your leadership to decide what "talent management" really means in your organization.

Ultimately, your organization's culture and history with workforce issues will determine what labels best support your efforts to maximize future workforce and leadership capabilities. In some organizations, "human capital" will be viewed as "too impersonal," while "workforce planning" may be seen as code for "downsizing" or "outsourcing."[18]

(continued)

Given the pros and cons of each term, and the preferences revealed by top managers in our research, we use *talent management* throughout the book because it is generally understood to cover most of the practical activities executives are trying to influence: recruitment, development, performance improvement, employee engagement, and retention of high-performing employees. But when we use the term, we also mean to include leadership development activities, as well as those commonly labeled "strategic workforce planning."

Define Your *Real* Role

Executives seeking to effectively implement talent management strategies might not know specifically *what* to do or *how* to do it. The vast majority of senior managers come from finance, operations, marketing, or sales disciplines, and they have had little exposure to the human capital challenges facing organizations today.[19] One former utility company CEO conceded, "I was general counsel and then served as CFO, so I had no training in leadership or management disciplines when I took over." By default, leaders like this must rely on a combination of their HR and organization development teams, plus middle managers, to generate the right mix of skills and future leaders for the organization.

We assume you want to have a positive impact on the capabilities of your workforce and leadership team. Unfortunately, many executives don't have a clear understanding of the tasks they should not delegate when it comes to talent management. That's where this book can help, by describing the senior manager's *real job* in developing future workforce and leadership capabilities. It shows specifically how leaders should do that job. With chapters on identifying strategic talent risks, how to evaluate current processes and practices, evaluating proposed solutions, and measuring results, this book reduces the uncertainty about the role of top managers in implementing talent strategies. And it will teach you how to evaluate whether or not you are doing the job well.

Challenges of Strategic Talent Management

In sectors as diverse as health care, energy, aerospace and defense, manufacturing, high tech, and government, talent management has become an overriding concern in recent years. Even organizations that seem to have more stable workforces today will find that demographic changes and recruiting challenges from other sectors are putting unexpected pressure on their ability to sustain and develop a highly skilled talent pool in the years ahead. Top executives who fail to confront this emerging threat—of growing competition for skilled professionals and capable younger leaders—will increasingly be held accountable for jeopardizing the future viability of their organizations. In the long term, organizations will find they cannot compete effectively in a global, technology-intensive economy unless their top executives know how to lead when it comes to strategic talent management.

This book gives you frameworks and tools for meeting this leadership challenge. It will show you how to translate your beliefs about the importance of investing in talent into concrete actions that directly affect business performance.

For Talent Management and HR Business Partners

How Talent Management Builds
Credibility with Business Leaders

The Executive Guide to High-Impact Talent Management is designed to teach top executives and business line leaders how to be better customers for talent management initiatives. We also intend it to help talent management and HR professionals work more effectively with senior line leaders whose goal is to develop a workforce and leadership team ready to meet future challenges.

Here are ways that you can use this chapter to help line executives collaborate with you on talent management efforts:

- **Define "talent management" for your organization.** As an HR or talent management professional, start by clearly defining what you mean by "talent management," or whatever term you choose to use in your organization. The scope of this concept can vary widely from one organization to the next. Whatever you choose to include—managing the entire employee life cycle, leadership development, succession planning, and so on—keep working to clarify that definition both for leaders in line and functional management roles and for your colleagues in talent management and human resources.
- **Be realistic about talent management in your organization.** How does your organization compare to our examples of alarm, overconfidence, and denial in this chapter? Do your primary business sponsors want to be innovators in talent management? Or would they prefer to implement traditional programs that have succeeded in other com-

panies? Knowing their inclination will help you present appropriate options.

- **Focus on the end goal of talent management.** Don't limit your thinking to how many programs you've implemented or the results of employee engagement surveys. Always frame the talent management work you're doing relative to the business problem you're solving. What language do you hear your top managers using to describe the talent problems they face? How are you building programs directly connected to solving those problems?

- **Seek out advocates in the business.** Part of becoming a true "business partner" involves building credible relationships with your internal customers. Keep your eye out for businesspeople who understand that talent management underpins the execution of business strategy. Find ways to collaborate on solutions with these colleagues in the business lines.

- **Help your line executives define their roles.** In one recent meeting between a C-level executive and his talent management staff, the senior leader got so exasperated in the middle of the conversation that he said, "Can someone tell me what you want me to do?" Adapt the tools in this book and present them to your internal customers so they can proactively play their parts in developing the workforce and leadership capabilities the organization needs. This may require you to lead them. That is what the executive in this example was asking for, and it is a role you should be prepared to play.

- **Learn about best practices and connect with colleagues.** Find links to our website at http://www.HighImpact TalentManagement.com and start connecting and sharing information with others.

2

An Executive Framework for Talent Management

If you have limited time to spend on the complexities of talent management, you need a context for decision making and a structure that focuses on the essential steps for developing future workforce and leadership capabilities. Start with a focus on the connection between your business strategy and the talent outcomes you hope to achieve. Then, as the leader, you can efficiently support your talent management staff at key steps along the way. Working with the framework outlined in this chapter, you can be more confident your workforce and leadership team is ready to execute your business strategy. Using our seven-part executive framework, you can:

- Do your part to set clear expectations for your organization's talent needs.
- Articulate the organization's cultural and operational norms that should shape talent needs.
- Diagnose why current talent management or leadership development initiatives are off base, redundant, or even counterproductive.
- Test future talent management plans to ensure they will use limited resources wisely.

This framework is comprehensive, yet relatively simple, and highly adaptable to your specific situation. It can support executive decision making in a range of scenarios. Do any of the following situations sound familiar?

Not Sure Where to Start on Talent Management

The new CEO of a major physicians group was frustrated to find her human resources department didn't think of employees as assets. "There were so many things missing in HR," she said. "They were trying to be compliance officers and policy people, but they weren't strategic. They had no sense of the competitive market they were in." This chief executive found stable HR systems but no talent development programs at any level in the organization. That included no career development planning, no identification of high-potential employees, and no meaningful performance management system. The only initiatives relevant to talent were focused on recruiting physician specialists. "We simply weren't leveraging our people," said this CEO, who was starting from scratch in developing talent management processes.

For this chief executive, underlying attitudes about employees were the problem. But sometimes nothing is being done to manage talent because the organization hasn't been big enough, long enough to warrant building the needed infrastructure. For example, a startup software company had grown to 150 employees before its leaders began to realize that better onboarding, management development, and succession planning were going to be necessary to support continued growth.

For organizations with no history of a talent management plan, HR or talent management staff will often try to address particular capability or skill gaps with one-time programs. In these situations the executives are often just grateful that *something* is being done. For example, a busy VP of operations in the software company approved funding for six new positions but didn't ask who would be reviewing résumés and screening applicants by phone to create a short list of candidates. He later found out that the hiring managers were so busy that they delegated these initial tasks to the group's administrative assistant. This shortsighted approach risked turning off the best candidates and delayed the start dates of much-needed new employees. When the new hires arrived, no further thought had been given to bringing them up to speed. Management's thinking was, "Just get them in here, and we'll work it out."

As this example shows, taking individual steps, such as opening employee requisitions to address specific talent needs, can seem like a good idea. But this activity often targets only part of the issue and gives executives a false sense of security that "the problem is solved." By using our framework for talent management, leaders can quickly look at the big picture for a particular talent issue and increase their chances that the end result will be a skilled staff and future leaders, ready to do the job—not just a "completed" talent management program.

Urgently Needing Talent Management

Sometimes the need for new talent initiatives becomes compelling for top management but the path forward is unclear.

This was the case for the CEO of a commercial insurance company who saw his business change rapidly. The company had grown tremendously in recent years, but now the market was saturated as competitors caught up, and sales were declining. The chief executive knew his company had to reinvent itself by offering a much broader line of financial services. Succeeding in new markets, however, required new technical capabilities. It also required leaders who could manage more strategically and work across organizational boundaries to shape the broader company agenda. These competencies didn't exist in the firm's current leadership team, and the CEO needed help building them.

Like the insurance executive, the head of a manufacturing division of an electronics design firm faced a broad strategic need. He knew that labor costs in Asia were often at least 50 percent cheaper than in the United States, and any growth in his organization should probably happen there. Since he planned to maintain a domestic presence, he would have employees spanning multiple physical, linguistic, and cultural divides. This manufacturing executive needed to clarify what work would be sent to Asia and determine how to ensure that his workers there would be skilled enough to do the job.

In organizations like this insurance company and manufacturing division, it is important to follow a structured approach when diagnosing and responding to the talent implications of such broad strategic challenges. By working through the steps from aligning business strategy, developing a holistic plan, implementing the plan, and finally to evaluating and measuring its success, leaders can oversee talent management programs more likely to address underlying business needs. Using our framework, executives can move beyond choosing point solutions, such as more training or a new organization chart or an outsourcing vendor, to a more consolidated view of talent management initiatives.

Sophisticated Talent Management in Place with Unclear Results

A growing number of companies today have extensive talent management processes in place. This means for many leaders it can become a little too easy to "check the box" when it comes to thinking they have talent and leadership development issues under control. But it's seldom as easy as that, and even companies such as General Electric, long idolized for its successful leadership development practices, have discovered this fact.

Reacting to a $200 billion drop in its market cap during the 2008–2009 recession, GE was forced to rethink the firm's talent management strategy. CEO Jeffrey Immelt felt compelled to reconsider GE's $1 billion annual investment in talent development. One question was whether it still made sense to take people out of their jobs for weeks at a time to teach them new skills in a corporate "top-down, university model of training."[1] Even organizations like GE that have historically been the gold standard for talent management need leaders willing to continually question whether their existing processes will produce the workforce and leadership capabilities needed to be competitive in the future.

These reevaluations of existing talent management processes are especially important when a company dramatically changes its business strategy or organizational structure. Our framework provides a quick way of reviewing key elements of your existing talent strategy to make sure they align in support of whatever new situation your company is encountering. For example, a major food manufacturer recently moved to a decentralized structure so business units now have their own P&Ls. This means R&D and other functional staff now report directly to business unit heads instead of to centralized corporate management. In this situation, the framework helps surface new talent-related questions that leaders should be asking, such as the following:

- Does the decentralized structure create any new talent-related risks (such as attrition or succession planning)? How do we make sure our talent-related risk priorities are still valid in the new organizational structure?
- How will we monitor and manage the inevitable shortages of talent in some areas when a core team is decentralized, since not every team will be able to have the "best resource" available?
- Does the decentralized structure change the way we should deliver our talent management initiatives? For example, how is career planning affected in R&D? Will there be resistance to moving senior R&D leaders across business units to gain critical experience, and if so, how should we address it?
- Do we need to change what we are measuring to evaluate talent initiatives more effectively in the decentralized structure?

The Talent Management Challenge for Executives

Chances are you can identify with one of the scenarios discussed in this chapter. Whatever your situation, it is probably hard to tell whether your company or business unit is actually developing a ready workforce and leadership team or just running a lot of talent management programs. All you may know is that these programs cost a lot, and your managers complain about how much time it takes to comply with these talent processes. No matter what brings talent issues to your attention, the potential responses often seem unclear, complicated, and costly. Here's an example of what happens when talent management goes wrong.

At a charity lunch, a senior manager for one of the world's biggest technology companies sat at a table with a bright, articulate, experienced project manager who seemed like a perfect fit for his company. He mentioned that his company was hiring and asked whether she'd considered interviewing there. Her response shocked him: "I thought I wanted to work there until I actually went for an interview. I was run around by the scheduling process, treated to a hodgepodge of unprepared interviewers, and left hanging for two weeks without any follow-up. When I finally got an offer letter, I decided to decline. I'd never want to work for a company that treats people that way."

Most executives would read this as a horror story. And for this high-tech company, it was. The firm had many openings to fill and was struggling with a lack of project managers. Subordinates in this company needed to understand the central importance of recruiting to achieve the business strategy, to appreciate the need for project managers, and to coordinate talent management solutions that attracted and retained outstanding candidates. In this case, the company's ability to deliver its product and to continue growing depended on filling a wide variety of jobs. Without successful recruiting and coordinated talent management programs, the company would not be able to reach this goal.

The recruiting process, however, might not be so important at another company in a different industry. If, for example, the leader in this story had been hiring only a handful of people, as compared to the numerous project managers needed, perhaps it could be argued that recruiting wasn't strategic enough to warrant this executive's attention. It is possible the leader wanted his talent management time and resources focused more on training and development of current employees than recruiting new ones.

Whatever the situation, the executive had an obligation to ask simple questions to assess the status of the highest priority talent management activities. If the recruiting process was identified as a critical component of the organization's talent management strategy, he could ask about the experience of candidates from sourcing through their first year on the job and probably would have uncovered any major issues, such as a haphazard recruiting and interviewing process. If the talent management strategy was more focused on training and development, he could examine the change in employees' knowledge and performance from one year to the next. Either way, executives need to learn when they must wade into the tactical issues about talent and when it is acceptable to take a more hands-off approach.

With the assumption that you have limited time for talent management, we have designed the framework in the following section to help you look under the covers of your talent management strategy. We assume that, in most cases, what you want is for talent management to be done well, and for you to be left out of it as much as possible. The approach we've taken is to allow you to analyze and vet the information you receive from your talent management staff to make sure you're confident they can deliver. Be aware, though, that the problems you uncover with this process may well start with you. Throughout the framework, we'll show how you as a leader can efficiently do your part to ensure talent management is on track.

A Strategic Framework for Action

Effective talent management strategies require a customized, multifaceted approach and a long-term commitment. For some organizations, the challenges of talent management will focus on a small set of burning issues, such as succession planning for the leadership team, effective onboarding of a new generation of engineers, or reinventing the performance management system. For others, like the physicians group CEO, talent management represents relatively uncharted territory. Or it can mean that a set of mature processes and practices need to be reevaluated and possibly reinvented, as GE's CEO discovered. No matter what your situation, the framework has seven critical success factors (CSFs) that will determine how successful you are in maximizing your investments in talent management. These seven CSFs, which will be dealt with in subsequent chapters, are outlined briefly in Figure 2.1.

1. Align Business and Talent Strategies by Clarifying the Big Picture

Chapter 3 focuses on why all decisions about managing talent must start in the context of the business strategy. More important, the chapter shows that communicating strategy alone isn't enough. Your staff also needs to be able to articu-

FIGURE 2.1   Executive Framework for Talent Management

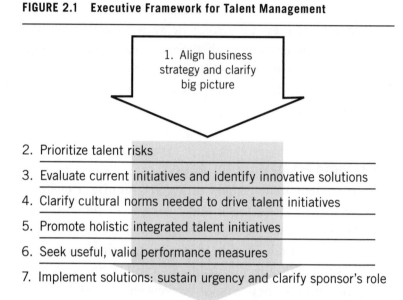

2. Prioritize talent risks

3. Evaluate current initiatives and identify innovative solutions

4. Clarify cultural norms needed to drive talent initiatives

5. Promote holistic integrated talent initiatives

6. Seek useful, valid performance measures

7. Implement solutions: sustain urgency and clarify sponsor's role

late a more detailed understanding of the evolving strategic context in which your firm is operating—what we call the big picture. While everyone involved may know the importance of aligning business strategy and talent management processes, *how* you actually do this is much less clear. In addition to using the big picture questions in Chapter 3, we will show in Chapter 10 why the evolving dynamics of who owns the talent management problem makes it essential to regularly realign talent initiatives with business strategy. The complexities brought on by increased globalization, rapid technology improvements, and the changing talent pool make alignment an ongoing challenge today. But it is also the strategic lever where leaders can have the greatest impact. That's why it is central to the first and last elements in our framework.

2. Identify and Prioritize Capability Gaps and Talent-Related Risks

Aligning strategy and talent provides decision-making guidance at a high level, but the organization also needs to know specifically where to focus its talent management resources. Prioritizing these investments can only occur after specific talent-related risks are exposed and evaluated. Whether it's replacing the capabilities of a veteran sales executive, minimizing the threat of losing key technical experts to competitors, reversing declining productivity among a rash of new hires, or addressing a dangerously thin pipeline of future leaders, top managers play a critical role in making sure these risks are identified and managed appropriately. Executives who let their organization skip this step are likely to end up investing in talent management solutions that don't support the business strategy. Chapter 4 provides practical tools for going beyond competency models to surface and manage capability gaps and their strategic, tactical, and operational talent-related risks.

3. Evaluate Current Initiatives and Identify Innovative Solutions

In our research we've found that evaluating the current state of talent programs is an obvious step that is rarely taken.

Many top managers don't know what questions they should be asking subordinates to assess the payoff of current investments in talent. Many don't even know the full scope of what is being done. One C-level executive at a public utility said that he didn't believe anyone in his organization could provide a comprehensive list of all the talent-related programs going on in any given month. Can you get quick answers to the following questions: How many different ways are your new hires being onboarded? How many formal or informal "mentoring" programs do you have? How many different consulting firms are working on talent problems, and is anyone coordinating them? Instead of responding passively to talent initiatives often sponsored by HR, leaders need to ensure that these offerings are, at the very least, available in a list so that the relationships between the various efforts can be properly assessed. Chapter 5 provides tools for taking inventory and evaluating current talent programs in a variety of different situations.

Leaders also should be aware of the latest thinking about creative solutions being used by others. Is your organization applying the best Web technologies to enhance the productivity of your young staff? What techniques for accelerating leadership development should you consider? Are you applying the best tools for transferring knowledge from retiring experts? Top managers don't need to get too deeply into the details when it comes to learning about the latest talent management solutions. But those who don't at least educate themselves enough to ask thoughtful questions about current solutions run the risk of rubber-stamping programs that are exciting and expensive but don't hit the mark. While this topic could be a book in itself, Chapters 6 and 7 provide a glimpse of some of the types of creative solutions being used to manage talent today. These chapters should give you enough vocabulary, interesting examples, and thoughtful questions to engage and challenge your talent management team.

4. Clearly State Cultural Norms That Should Drive Talent Initiatives

This is another powerful step that is rarely taken for lack of a simple way to do it. In fact, companies frequently fail to articulate their existing cultural norms that influence talent management outcomes. Just as there often are assumed and unstated ideas on business strategy, organizations often leave the understanding of culture vague and unclear. This is ironic because supporting and promoting a productive culture is one of the most important things executives do. Only when you communicate your cultural expectations can you check to see whether talent solutions are supporting them.

When we talk of using culture to drive talent management in Chapter 5, we're talking about broad beliefs and directions that typically can be laid out on a continuum. For example:

- Consistent and centralized leadership and management practices versus an independent and autonomous approach to leadership and management
- Promoting most of the next generation of managers and executives from within the organization versus hiring from outside
- The desire to reduce the population of more experienced, potentially more expensive employees versus a commitment to actively retain longtime workers and to maintain relationships with former employees

- The plan to lay off surplus talent as quickly as possible versus the goal of maintaining a steady headcount
- The strategy of growing by hiring versus the strategy of growing through acquisition of other companies

Executives often want to influence the culture of their organizations but lack a simple way to do that. Articulating these principles is an opportunity to shape your culture, while also setting expectations for your talent management staff. Chapter 5 will give you more ideas about how to use this concept in decision making about talent management initiatives.

5. Promote Holistic Integrated Talent Initiatives

One of the most common mistakes in managing talent is failing to acknowledge that different activities must work together in order to achieve desired outcomes. For example, recruiting, developing, and retaining the most innovative designers, inventors, and researchers in your firm is not likely to be achieved merely through an adequate performance review process and sufficient compensation. Other factors could include specialized internships, collaborative idea-sharing or problem-solving platforms, rotational assignments, mentoring, access to external training opportunities, hosting industry events, and so on. Each one of these efforts could be led by a different group and could potentially be competing for time, resources, and the attention of participants. This step in the framework reminds leaders that they must look for integrated approaches to managing talent, not one-time solutions. Action steps for developing a more holistic, integrated approach are addressed in Chapter 9.

6. Seek Useful, Valid Performance Measures

Executives also play a key role in setting expectations about how the effects of talent initiatives should be measured. For example, when the president of a major pharmaceutical company was reviewing a proposed executive development program, he stopped subordinates in their tracks by asking, "How are you going to know if their behavior changes?" This forced his talent management staff to develop an evaluation strategy for the initiative that included a baseline analysis, so they could show improvement. While important, this executive's curiosity was unfortunately unusual. More leaders need to ask how investments in talent management will improve the ability of participants to understand and do their jobs and deliver on the organization's strategy. Action steps for developing essential measures are described in Chapter 8.

7. Implement Talent Solutions: Sustain Urgency and Clarify Roles

Depending on the size of the organization, top managers can be relatively removed from the day-to-day implementation of talent programs. But they still have an essential role to play in the success of these initiatives. One of the key tasks for any leader is clearly defining his or her own role as sponsor of a particular talent program. Are you the project owner, or is someone else accountable for it? Are you also running this talent initiative, or have you delegated that task to someone else? These are critical questions to be addressed.

Another difficult task called out in the framework is the need to create and sustain urgency around talent management efforts. Executives who don't understand their roles in effective implementation doom talent initiatives to failure. Chapter 9 shows three specific things leaders must do to support key implementation tasks.

No Shortcuts to Effective Talent Management

Ultimately, every organization's approach to managing talent will involve a unique combination of processes, practices, and policies. But the success of these efforts is largely determined by how effectively leaders execute the seven steps outlined in our framework. Even if your firm's talent management processes are relatively sophisticated today, they almost certainly can be improved by reflecting on your performance in each step of the framework. The most common mistake top managers make is focusing on only a few of the elements we have described.

Success in managing highly skilled talent in today's business environment requires clear priorities, passion, and perseverance. For leaders this framework shows ways to be more effective, and the first lesson is that there are no shortcuts when it comes to maximizing your talent management investments.

3

Aligning Talent Investments to Support Business Strategy

Common sense says organizations should hire, develop, and retain people who will help them achieve their business goals most cost effectively.

The problem is few executives seem to know *how* to intentionally create this alignment between an organization's strategic objectives and its talent management efforts. Therefore the benefits described from such an alignment often are not achieved. Strategic misalignment costs organizations millions of dollars every year because it severely undermines firms' abilities to achieve long-term performance goals. Ineffective performance management systems and onboarding processes that don't maximize the productivity of new hires result from strategic mismatches that leaders will sometimes live with for years. This misalignment can seriously undermine performance.

The solution to lack of alignment is deceptively simple, but it may not be what you expect. It requires communicating not just strategy but also strategic context. Then testing—that is, asking questions—must take place to verify that your talent management team understands the strategic big picture well enough to apply it to hiring, staff development, and retention decisions. By creating a feedback loop between top management and those implementing talent initiatives, you greatly increase the likelihood that your investments will pay off.

To quickly forge a closer connection between strategic goals and talent management processes, this chapter will show:

- How business strategies create very different talent management needs in similar businesses
- What creating alignment really means
- Why traditional ideas about communicating strategy are often ineffective
- How to use strategy so that it positively affects decision making about talent management

Connecting Strategy to Talent Needs: Two Approaches, One Industry

In industries that run on highly skilled workers, it is easy to assume that talent needs are similar from one company to the next. This is not true. Even companies that are reaching into the same pool of talent, recruiting for similar skill sets, and operating within the same geographic area can find—once they apply the strategy filter—that their needs and requirements for talent are remarkably different.

Two real examples, both from the video gaming industry, show how firms in the same business drawing on the same talent pool can require radically different approaches to talent management. Only by making explicit the talent demands of their own strategy can leaders in these firms expect subordinates to make smart decisions about staffing and leadership development.

A major video game developer we'll call Distributed Video Corp. (DVC) set a clear strategy several years ago. DVC said it would grow to dominate its category by partnering heavily on content, licensing existing brands wherever possible, and quickly getting new products to market. Furthermore, DVC would grow the organization by acquiring successful smaller game companies within its genre. Almost without exception these new acquisitions would continue to operate as though nothing had changed. Autonomy was so valued, in fact, that regular communication between these acquired companies was never encouraged at Distributed Video. They would remain in their original locations with their own brand identities to follow their own processes and creative directions. Headquarters would simply provide the production, publication, and distribution of the acquired companies' products.

At roughly the same time, a second major video game developer that we'll call Central Video set a very different strategy. Central's approach was to grow its business by developing new content based on already successful themes, iterating with new releases annually. Little content would come from outside. Central Video would grow the organization by hiring and managing individual people working in franchises at a handful of larger, central locations. Each franchise would develop and iterate on successful titles, creating next-generation graphics and platforms to maintain and grow its market share. Everyone in the company would follow a set game development process and use proprietary tools. The corporate brand was central, and there were distinct "look and feel" similarities that encouraged customers of one product to pick up the next.

Although both examples are in the same industry, competing for the same customer, they need a very different mix of talent to execute their distinct strategies. What are the differences that drive talent management for each?

Distributed Video's strategy created a need for a highly decentralized organization that encourages retention of the "garage startup" mentality of its acquired companies. It resists standardization in the creative process and seeks to work much like a publisher works with authors: pick good writers and good topics and then stay relatively hands-off until the finished product is completed and thrown over the wall. Then the publisher takes the product and gets it into the market, while the creative team returns to the drawing board to start the process all over. Creativity is fostered by the lack of constraints.

Central Video's strategy is much different. Plenty of creativity is required, but everyone in the division follows a set game development process and uses proprietary tools. Efficiency, consistency, and staying on brand are required to make the strategy work. Each team must go through defined gates as it marches toward completion. Many central services are standardized to take care of more mundane tasks, so creative teams spend far fewer hours cleaning up messes made by a lack of process—leaving more time to make their products fun. Creativity is fostered by removing the chaos.

Now, take a step back and imagine the onboarding or leadership development program for a company that insists on autonomy versus one that expects a relatively strict adherence to central command. Imagine the different questions a recruiter should ask in screening candidates for cultural fit for one company versus the other. Imagine the talent needed to develop the internal infrastructure for Central Video versus maintaining the loose-knit coalition at DVC. And imagine the kinds of executives (current and future) needed to grow through acquisition versus through the development of teams and franchises.

If talent management was not aligned with strategy in this example, the results could be very expensive. For example, if onboarding at Central Video failed to quickly teach new employees the rules of the relatively strict processes, they could spend weeks or months producing work that would eventually prove unusable. This not only wastes time but also is demoralizing to the new employees and likely to increase turnover. Such a situation is potentially devastating to the creative process and game development. Alternatively, knowledge transfer at Distributed Video is all about encouraging a bit of creative chaos, with all mentoring controlled at the local level in order to support local strategy. If project management training at Distributed Video failed to help the autonomous companies continue to improve quality and hit deadlines (despite their different cultures), millions of dollars could be lost with each late product release.

In this narrative, it is easy to see that these are two very different strategies, each with its merits and potential risks and each requiring quite different talent management programs. If you were an executive in either of these companies, the whole picture would undoubtedly be clear to you. But imagine being in the trenches at one of these companies, just trying to do your job: hiring, developing, and retaining the right people. Employees in this situation know that their "culture" and "mission" are unique, but they are unable to articulate how or why. They often find themselves uttering a generic battle cry like "we hire smart people who can get the job done." These managers are capable, but they haven't internalized the business strategy. As a result, they don't have a clear understanding of *what* talent is needed and *why*.

Secrets to Aligning Talent Management with Business Strategy

In our experience, to get the results they need from talent management, executives must be good customers and *say what they want*. This means they must continually communicate strategic context (for example, key competitors, performance measures, critical business initiatives), *in addition to the strategy itself*, to managers at all levels of the organization. In the end, alignment means that even frontline employees (including recruiters, trainers, and compensation experts) are able to articulate key aspects of the firm's strategic context and how it affects specific talent initiatives.

Leaders who successfully link strategy and talent management adhere to five principles. Specifically, they:

1. Understand and teach the rest of the organization what "alignment" means
2. Recognize the critical role they must play in leading alignment discussions
3. See the limits of just "communicating" strategy and go beyond that
4. Recognize the secret to alignment is communicating relevant strategic context, also known as the big picture
5. Link subordinates' understanding of strategic context directly to talent initiatives

What Is Alignment?

To ensure that talent management advances strategic objectives, employees at all levels must understand what you mean by alignment. As we use the term, *alignment* is a clear relationship between the business strategy and talent management that supports effective decision making about talent initiatives. This means executives must explicitly articulate the strategy so that managers at all levels can clearly understand the implications for hiring, development, and retention. One former oil company chief executive explained it this way: "The most important thing a leader can do to communicate is to keep the bigger picture in focus, to set the context . . . to explain or reconcile the complexities that cloud the overall picture of what's important and why."[1]

Providing strategic context is critical. Unfortunately, top managers often talk about the mythical strategic "big picture" as though it is obvious to everyone. We say, "She gets it" or "He doesn't get it." "Getting the big picture" can be essential for promotion, and "not getting the big picture" can be a reason to fire someone.

But it is rarely clear what we really mean when we talk about the big picture. In particular, long-established teams often presume a shared understanding about the strategic context of their work. Executives are prone to believe that since colleagues in the boardroom get the big picture, so does everyone all the way down to the front line. In truth, as a manager in a major consumer products company observed, "Our executives may nod confidently when we talk about the big picture, but I don't think even they would all agree on what it means."

To ensure understanding of strategic intent, test how well your team gets the big picture. To measure the alignment of strategy and talent processes, ask two simple questions about the strategy/talent connection:

1. Can everyone responsible for managing talent answer questions about the strategic big picture—and are everyone's answers similar? (See the section "The Secret to Alignment: Communicating the Big Picture" later in this chapter for details.)
2. Does every talent management program directly map to the business strategy, solving for an explicit need? (If not, see Table 3.1 on page 61 for ideas on how to make those links.)

Executives Must Play a Leading Role in Creating Alignment

Once you've agreed on what it means to align business strategy and talent management efforts, make sure you're not the barrier to fixing what could turn out to be a costly problem. It's as if your car's wheels were badly out of alignment for months on end. Your ride may still be functioning, but you're beating the hell out of your tires and continually fighting steering problems. Whether the neglect is benign ("I've gotten used to the status quo") or active ("I don't want to pay for it"), you don't want to be the reason your talent strategy—or your car—is not performing as well as it should. Here's how to make sure you are supporting the alignment of strategy and talent management:[2]

1. Don't delegate discussions about strategy and talent management to middle managers. The execution of talent management activities is tactical, but ensuring that these activities support the business strategy is a key executive function. "You've got to attack talent issues

on a disciplined basis," said one former utility company CEO. "You must ask, 'How is this talent investment going to make us more effective? Show me.' Is it net income, ROE, more favorable customer satisfaction surveys? How is what you're doing in HR going to improve performance? Sometimes the correlation may not be direct, but requiring that the causal connection be made is important."

2. Give thinking and talking about strategy the same attention you devote to operational problems. Unfortunately, as one quality guru puts it, it's more satisfying to brag about "killing alligators" than it is to explain how you deftly handled a baby alligator before it could bite.[3] However, evaluating alignment is not merely about trying to find the right answer in a crisis (e.g., firing or transferring an ineffective manager, that is, killing alligators); it is about asking the right questions to prevent problems (e.g., preventing unproductive talent investments, that is, preventing the bite). Which activity is less risky and less costly? Think of discussions about the link between strategy and talent management as preventative maintenance—a chance to make sure the organization is making the right investments.

3. Alignment occurs at multiple levels of the organization. Be clear about what level you're concerned with:
   - A corporate-level business strategy and talent needs across multiple, diversified business units
   - The strategy of an individual business unit with focused talent management for that group
   - A functional strategy like IT, supply chain, or finance

No matter what level or which unit you are focused on, make sure all participants understand your priority when managing talent. For example, a CIO or division general manager may have very different goals for developing high potentials than the CEO. Make sure your colleagues are clear about which strategy you are serving.

4. Acknowledge the difficulty of creating alignment and measuring success. Don't avoid these conversations just because they're hard. Talent management needs that directly affect strategy pose multiple challenges and require multipronged solutions. And often there is no quick way to measure the success of decisions intended to solve them.[4]

Recognize the Limits of "Communicating" Strategy to Create Alignment

Leaders produce a wide range of messages they call "strategy": informal ideas not written down anywhere or operational plans that reflect implied strategy but do not clearly state it. At the other extreme, some firms have used high-priced consultants to create 200-page strategy manifestos detailing every possible permutation. No matter where your organization is on this continuum, communicating strategic objectives means different things to different leaders. We've identified a continuum of strategy messages from extremely broad on one end to precise and operational on the other. In different situations, each of these strategies is considered clear by an executive team. What then is the *right* level of detail for creating alignment with talent management efforts?

How abstract or operational is your organization's strategy? What is the right level of detail for you? As you review the following four examples, imagine your talent management team trying to make decisions based on this information.

We Just Give 'em the Bullets

Consider this language from a big box retailer:

Our business strategy is to deliver sustainable and profitable growth by:

- *Enhancing the Core: Making our existing stores the best they can be*
- *Extending the Business: Adding adjacent businesses where appropriate*
- *Expanding Our Markets: Opening new stores, new formats, and new markets*

This strategy may sound great at first, but in truth it would make as much sense to almost any retail business as to the big box retailer. It's hard to tell what business this company is in. Imagine trying to figure out what kind of talent management programs your firm needs to support this so-called strategy.

More Bullets, More Detail

Here is a strategy from a leading wireless services provider:

- *Regain number one net growth leadership*
- *Lifetime profitable customer relationships*
- *Improve network and handset service reliability*
- *Bring our product richness into the home*
- *Be America's best place to work*

This list gets to some critical points for moving the company forward, such as a focus on reliability, but it still does not give real direction. Imagine recruiting, hiring, training, evaluating, and supporting a workforce and leadership team to implement this strategy. How would your business unit and talent managers know they were on target?

Lots of Details, Some Strategic Direction

Baker & McKenzie's more detailed strategy moves down the specificity continuum and begins to suggest a logical direction for talent management. An excerpt from this global law firm's strategy follows:

1. To achieve market preeminence by building upon unparalleled international capabilities through: deeper penetration of major clients; growth of our core practice areas; and greater industry specialization.
2. To develop the firm in a systematic way so each office is able to support multinational clients and global strategy and excel and prosper in its local market.
3. To align the firm's organizational, financial, and management structures more effectively with its strategic objectives. [emphasis added]5

This strategy provides guidance for talent management efforts. For example, the underlined phrases could be used to guide talent management processes and programs. As you read the following analysis, ask yourself: Does your strategy provide *at least* this level of direction?

Some implications of these strategic objectives for talent management are:

- **"Deeper penetration of major clients."** With fewer, larger clients, there is a need to intimately understand the clients' core businesses at the international level. Deeper penetration will allow for both better service and increased opportunities with each client. Those responsible for talent management could work to define the expected "depth of client knowledge" required for any employee working on an account. Then they could design programs (such as onboarding, mentoring, and training) to ensure that those with deep knowledge are sharing that information effectively.
- **"Growth of our core practice areas."** Every office should have a known set of skills required to deliver on its core practice areas. Talent managers could help define the skills needed in each practice area, analyze current skill levels, assess the risks of insufficient bench strength, and develop a plan to bridge the gap.
- **"Greater industry specialization."** The firm must have a critical mass of employees who are fluent in the issues of their clients' industries. The talent management efforts could include an audit of industry expertise within each region (see the Knowledge Silo Matrix in Chapter 4 for an example), an analysis of the risk of insufficient bench strength, and a plan to develop a baseline of industry knowledge.

This analysis suggests that Baker & McKenzie's strategy language could guide talent management activities. If strategy is intended to show both where we're headed and where we're *not* headed, this level of detail is better than the others. Still, an executive who communicates this level of detail should not be overly confident that it will translate directly into a talent management plan. You still have to test to ensure you've been clear.

Very Detailed Strategy: Too Much Information?

Southwest Healthcare System (company disguised) provides yet more detail in its 30-page strategy document. The following excerpt illustrates the specificity provided for both strategy and tactics. At first glance, this appears to provide explicit direction for managing talent, but how should the talent management staff operationalize it?

Strategic Objective #1: Recruit and Select a Highly Skilled, Diverse Workforce

Tactics

- *Hire the right employees to achieve success*
- *Encourage and equip our existing workforce to serve as company advocates*
- *Analyze workforce trends to develop a recruitment strategy for key positions*
- *Establish relationships with select "feeder" institutions for desired talent:*
  - *Classroom presentations, college fairs, event sponsorships, and branding*
- *Strategically recruit outside our region as needed*
- *Continue focus on increasing diversity and inclusion of our workforce, including leaders, and measure results*
- *Develop a system and culture that encourages informational interviews with current employees and people interested in working for our organization*

Strategic Objective #2: Develop and Retain the Best Leaders

Tactics

- *Clearly communicate the roles and expectations of leaders through multiple vehicles including Leader Orientation and the Leadership Institute*
- *Systematically assess leaders' levels of engagement and developmental needs:*
  - *Encourage cross-department and -division moves*
  - *Promote involvement in external professional organizations*
- *Reinforce training and provide tools that strengthen leadership skills (e.g., having the courageous conversation, accountability, managing differences, crisis management, etc.)*
- *Encourage local rewards and recognition including more extensive use of toolkits to reinforce the value of demonstrating appreciation.*

This is just one portion of Southwest's strategy document. At first glance, this appears to provide explicit direction for managing talent. It seems to give as much guidance as anyone could want—until you try to put it into action. Where would you begin, given this level of detail? How does this strategic plan communicate priorities and guide the eventual activities outlined as tactics? How can Southwest Healthcare's leaders ensure that this document translates into effective talent management programs?

In reality, no matter how confident you are that your strategy is clear, there is still work to do in ensuring that your managers and talent team understand how to assess talent management efforts, as they take shape. The problem is that most strategies are not detailed enough to provide that framework, no matter how fat the binders or how fancy the PowerPoint slide deck. You can train every employee in the company to recite your 35-word strategy verbatim, or you can develop a 30-page document that leaves no stone unturned. But that isn't enough. An important step in creating alignment is recognizing that simply getting staff to recite strategy back like a parrot is inadequate. How can you be certain that your talent management staff and line managers are making decisions and taking action that actually support strategic objectives?

The Secret to Alignment: Communicating the Big Picture

However you state your strategy, you need to give executives and employees the perspective they need to plan, prioritize, make decisions, and take action every day to clearly support strategic objectives. Here's a simpler way to look at it.

If everyone in your organization can answer a few questions in a way that maps to the strategy and sounds like what their manager says, then they "get the big picture." The converse is also true: those who cannot answer the questions in a way that maps to strategy and their manager's understanding prove they *don't* get the big picture.

This understanding rolls up all the way from receptionists to senior vice presidents. *Everyone* should be able to answer the big picture questions and sound like their bosses when doing so. You'll know your team gets the big picture and, consequently, the strategy, if they can answer the following questions and sound like you at the same time. As you read each one, ask yourself if answering the question incorrectly would change an employee's actions for the worse. If it does, keep it on the list. If not, remove it.

1. Who are the customers or customer segments we serve, listed in priority order?
2. What are the products or services we provide now, and which ones, if any, need to change as we implement the current strategy?
3. With whom (and in what priority) do we partner in delivering our products or services?
4. Who are our competitors (listed in priority order), why is each considered a threat, and what can we learn from them?
5. How do we measure our success now, and how might that change in the future?
6. What is the relevant history that affects current strategy?
7. Which environmental trends or issues (such as market, economic, societal, political, or environmental factors) are important to our strategy?
8. How does our organizational structure support our strategy?
9. What are three things your unit is doing to support the strategy?

For each of these big picture questions, there are right and wrong answers. The right answers change when the business strategy changes. Good people can be working very hard on the wrong activities if their answers to these questions are off base.

Link Big Picture Responses to Talent Initiatives

Testing direct reports and key talent management staff on strategic questions is important. It connects the firm's strategic context to each individual's objectives. Don't let this step slide. Keep testing until you get thoughtful, strategy-savvy answers.

For example, the CEO of a high-tech company found that his HR director could answer all these important questions with deep understanding. However, when he asked the director if her direct reports could speak cogently about strategy, she realized that this was not possible. This situation helped her recognize that her team was too focused on general-purpose HR practices and was not specifically targeting the strategic needs of the company. Today, HR staff members often want to be considered "business partners" with line management. But to truly fill this role, they must be able to answer the big picture questions relating to their organization's business strategy.

Once you have tested understanding, challenge talent managers to link their answers to specific talent initiatives. In our experience, many top managers avoid this step. "A lot of executives don't want to ask hard questions around something they see as soft, like leadership development," said one progressive talent management director in a pharmaceutical company. "They act as if it's easier just to show some activity around developing leaders and hope that people liked it. Then, eventually, maybe we'll see a change in behavior." The key to creating alignment is challenging your staff to think through the connections between specific talent initiatives and the organization's strategic context.

Table 3.1 shows how you can use the answers to these big picture questions to ensure your talent investments are on track. You can use these questions to test alignment, in particular, by listening to the answers to the questions in the third column of Table 3.1.

TABLE 3.1   Understanding the "Big Picture"

Big Picture Issue	Sample Talent Management Activity	Alignment Test Question	Sample Answers Showing Alignment
Who are our competitors?	Recruiting/ staffing	How does our recruiting effort position us against key competition?	We track candidates hired away from each competitor, our employees who've left to join a competitor, and offers extended to candidates who end up choosing a competitor. We use this data to win or maintain more of the best candidates.
Who is the customer?	Performance review	How do we reward employees who show a strong understanding of the customer?	In each review, employees are asked to name their highest priority internal and/or external customers and give examples of excellent service or work done that affects the customer experience. Their review score and compensation are affected by this information.

(continued)

TABLE 3.1   Understanding the "Big Picture" *(continued)*

Big Picture Issue	Sample Talent Management Activity	Alignment Test Question	Sample Answers Showing Alignment
What are our products or services?	Diversity	What products or service areas present the most critical need for new talent, and how is diversity helping us respond to that need?	Our strategy includes introducing our product into three new markets, and we use our diversity effort to ensure representatives of those three new markets are working in key roles across the organization.
Who are our most important partners?	Career development	What steps are we taking to clarify expectations and improve communication and information sharing between key partners?	We identified four outsource partners who play mission critical roles in our career development programs. We found no way for them to communicate *with each other* to improve how they serve/partner with us. We have now made introductions between them and encouraged them to learn from each other as well as from their counterparts inside our organization.
What are our success metrics?	Training	How does our training effort improve the focus on key performance indicators (KPI)?	Training can map each educational program back to a KPI and conducts follow-up with 30 percent of participants to track improvements on KPIs resulting from the programs.

Big Picture Issue	Sample Talent Management Activity	Alignment Test Question	Sample Answers Showing Alignment
What is the relevant history for our strategy?	Mentoring	How does your mentoring program ensure wisdom and tacit knowledge are transferred?	Mentors are trained to relate company history to strategic choices, and they can describe how the organization has changed over time and why.
Which environmental trends will impact our success?	Succession planning	How does your succession planning respond to the current economic situation, pipeline of available talent, and competitive threat?	We've analyzed our current succession plan for employees at risk. We've assessed data around likely turnover. We've compared our succession plans across divisions. We've surveyed employees who are currently in the pipeline.
Which environmental trends will impact our success?	Social media, communities of practice, affinity groups	In what ways are you facilitating a robust discussion of the day-to-day issues we face both now and in the near future?	We use internal social networking to present challenges the organization is facing so that employees can engage in the solution real-time and in the course of their regular jobs. The best ideas are floated up to senior management.

(continued)

TABLE 3.1   Understanding the "Big Picture" *(continued)*

Big Picture Issue	Sample Talent Management Activity	Alignment Test Question	Sample Answers Showing Alignment
What is your team doing to support the strategy?	Leadership development	How does your management training program ensure leaders can answer the big picture questions for their team?	We have a quarterly brown-bag lunch where we answer all the big picture questions explicitly and follow up with spot checks to ensure that managers and individual employees can answer the questions confidently.
All big picture questions	Onboarding	How does our onboarding program introduce our new employees to their roles in executing the strategy?	The onboarding program includes a 30-minute module explaining the critical role in understanding the big picture and training new hires to ask their managers to review the answers during the first week on the job. We spot-check 50 percent of all new hires within their first month on the job.

For example, Table 3.1 links the strategy question (in column 1), "Who are our competitors?" to specific activities (in column 4), in this case, tracking recruiting and retention in comparison to competitors. To see if your talent management staff is aligned with business strategy, you should be asking them questions (in column 3) about particular activities (column 2). To a question like "How does our recruiting effort position us against key competition?" you should look for an answer in column 4. Listen for answers that show a rational link between the shared understanding of your competitors and the way your recruitingw processes and practices help you succeed against competitors (assuming that is a relevant issue). The message to your talent management staff should be clear: *"If you can't answer these questions, your talent management programs are not aligned with our business strategy, and we're not going to fund or support them."*

How Cisco Uses the Big Picture

Cisco is a $37 billion company that communicates strategic context through big picture–type questions. CEO John Chambers is relentless in communicating the organization's corporate strategy and the relevant strategic context throughout the organization. This leading supplier of Internet networking gear has more than 65,000 employees and operates in 83 countries. Through its corporate communications organization, the firm has built an elaborate process to help employees understand where the business is going and what they should be doing to support it in that direction.

At Cisco, line executives meet regularly with talent management staff to discuss the talent implications of specific elements of the firm's current strategy, such as expanding market share in collaborative technologies. Executives are continually being challenged to translate the CEO's strategic objectives into more localized talent implications. Here are some questions Cisco uses:

- What is the competitive landscape for this particular business?
- Do we need smart people who can execute in this market? Or do we need more aggressive people who can go toe-to-toe with major competitors?
- Where is this business in its life cycle? Is it small and rapidly growing? Is it mature or a turnaround situation?

In reality, not all Cisco executives are naturally inclined to communicate the answers to these big picture questions. The CEO's leadership team is working to change this behavior. Another challenge is clarifying strategic context at lower levels in the organization. For example, one Cisco recruiter knew that increasing investments in "smart grid" technologies was a major strategic initiative. Management had communicated the strategy of pursuing new opportunities in the market for managing electrical power at the macro level.

For her, that meant knowing what kinds of projects related to "smart grid" were currently under way at Cisco that new employees might work on. The recruiter pursued an answer to this question from a senior project manager so she could provide more specifics for highly prized, career-minded job candidates. "It's one thing to have big strategic initiatives identified," said the recruiter. "But, at my level, job candidates want to know, 'What am I going to be doing?' So I better have an answer for that."

Cisco's leadership has demonstrated a commitment to communicating its strategy throughout the organization. It recognized that the need to align strategy with daily activities in talent management means going further than broadcasting a few key business objectives. It means encouraging employees at all levels to think about the context in which the strategy is being implemented. Alignment is an outgrowth of ongoing conversations between leaders and their employees.

Six Action Steps to Immediately Improve Alignment

When it comes to talent management, the executive's most important task is to make sure talent management is designed to create workforce and leadership capabilities that are clearly aligned with the organization's strategy. Many top managers are only able to review talent management activities once or twice a year. If that's your situation, here are a few things you can do immediately to make sure your talent management investments provide the best possible payoff.

1. Articulate your strategy and answer the big picture questions explicitly in the form of a white paper or 30-minute presentation.
2. Test your direct reports to ensure they have the same answers to big picture questions. *Don't assume others know about the strategy.*
3. Ask your head of HR or top talent management executive to explain how he or she is introducing the strategy and big picture to staff.
4. Insist on a plan to methodically communicate the big picture to *all* staff members. Ensure that the talent management team is able to connect programs to the big picture.
5. When reviewing budget requests, talent management project plans, reorganization plans, recruiting plans, headcount plans, and so on, ask yourself and others how each one of these plans will help execute your strategy.

Accept only proposals that can be tied back to the big picture.

6. Once you determine that a talent management effort can be tied to strategy, ask how that is being communicated to the participants of the program.

For Talent Management and HR Business Partners

If Necessary, Drive the Strategic Discussion

Although this book is intended to help senior executives work more productively with you, HR innovators can also use these tools and concepts to "manage up" and communicate effectively with line executives.

For HR staffers who want to work as true "business partners," understanding and internalizing business strategy is an important first step. This means that you not only need to be able to repeat your company's strategy statement, but also to describe the practical effects of that strategy. To be a business partner, you must prove that you understand the strategy well enough to develop the strong leaders and ready workforce needed to implement it.

Ideally, your line executives do a good job of helping everyone in your organization understand the strategy, but that isn't always the case. Perhaps your senior leaders aren't clearly communicating the big picture or checking to see that you and your team understand it. In that case, it's up to you to take action.

You can start by answering the big picture questions described in this chapter to make explicit your current understanding of the strategy. Answer the questions to the best of your ability in writing. Take time to detail your understanding of each question to really test the depth of your knowledge. Then, discuss these ideas with a trusted colleague in the business unit—someone who has credibility in the business and can help you see where your perceptions might differ from those of your senior leaders.

Next, schedule a meeting to describe your answers to the big picture questions to a senior manager or executive who is an internal customer on the business side. Ask the executive to respond and give you feedback on your answers. It's not enough to discuss strategy with other HR people. You need to have this conversation with people in the business units. Then, make sure your HR colleagues can answer the big picture questions as well. You gain credibility with your internal customers when you prove you're a student of the business issues they face. In addition, encourage the line executives you support to insist that the managers in their business units be able to answer the same big picture questions outlined in this chapter. There is nothing more powerful than getting everyone in the organization on the same page in terms of strategy. Answering the big picture questions is a straightforward and efficient way to do that.

4

Prioritizing Talent
Management Risks

R isk management has become a highly sophisticated process that is an increasingly popular concept with many executive teams. But leaders seldom think in terms of risk when it comes to workforce and leadership development, even though the effects of failing to manage talent-related risks can range from costly to catastrophic. To complicate matters, many of the methods used to analyze talent and other business risks today have proved to be ineffective and even counterproductive.[1] Given the difficulty of quantifying talent management problems, investments, and results, the challenge is to use risk management methodologies so they produce better outcomes, instead of just making managers feel better.

When it comes to talent management, a vague sense that things are "good" or "not good" is not enough. A clear understanding of strategic, tactical, and operational risks that affect your hiring, development, and retention of key employees is essential to evaluate the performance of your firm's existing talent management investments and to make good decisions as an executive sponsor.

Failing to effectively assess and mitigate the risks of not having a ready workforce and adequate leadership pipeline can create problems such as the following:

- Too little capacity, causing delays in product or service delivery and undermining the capacity for growth
- Too much capacity, leading to lower utilization rates and lower margins
- Too many specialists and not enough generalists when flexibility is required
- Quality problems because not enough employees are fully trained
- Increased attrition/turnover because key staff get frustrated and leave when they're not well deployed

This chapter will show you how to think effectively about prioritizing the most serious talent risk factors facing your organization. It will help you address four questions:

- What talent-related risks are likely to hurt your organization's performance?
- What is the likelihood these risks will occur?
- How can you determine the impact of specific talent-related risks on your business and future capabilities?
- Which talent risks are most critical to address today?

The Most Serious Talent Risk Factors

For our purposes, risk means exposure to unwanted talent-related outcomes that would prevent the organization from delivering expected results. Risk also implies the *probability* of something bad happening because of the presence of specific risk factors.[2]

When it comes to talent management, you first need to separate the actual risk factors from concerns about the likelihood they will produce specific negative outcomes. For example, consider the risk factor of having hired 30 percent of your sales force in the last year. In a company selling a limited number of simple products, this might not present a serious risk to overall performance, but in a high-tech firm with many complex products it would be a major threat to achieving sales goals. As you can see, the context of the situation matters a great deal.

To prioritize serious talent risks for your business, you must first identify the presence of specific risk factors. Five are most common:

- Shortage of essential talent
- High percentage of new hires
- Dissatisfied employees
- Shortage of talent in leadership pipeline
- Loss of critical skilled employees

Shortage of Essential Talent

Constant Contact provides e-mail marketing for small and medium-sized businesses. This company's sales revenues and workforce have consistently grown more than 30 percent annually in recent years. Constant Contact's leaders recognized that to achieve their aggressive growth objectives the company would need to successfully recruit and retain key technical specialists. The risk of failing to acquire new expertise in areas such as search engine optimization and

Internet marketing could pose a threat to the firm's strategic objectives.

To identify whether critical talent shortages pose a serious risk, your team should be able to answer these questions:

- What roles should we be most concerned about when recruiting to sustain future performance?
- Given competition in the market for talent, our geographic location, and the time it takes to develop adequate skills, what roles in our firm will be most difficult to fill?
- If not filled adequately, what roles will have the most negative impact on our organizational capabilities and performance?
- Given our strategic objectives and the anticipated changes in our workforce and leadership team, what assumptions are we making about the availability of critical talent in the marketplace? How have we tested these assumptions?

High Percentage of New Hires

One of the world's largest semiconductor manufacturers planned to shift its strategic focus from hardware to software solutions. To support this change in strategy and the expected explosive growth, this multinational firm planned to hire more than 700 new software engineers. While the engineering talent was expected to be available, top management did not pay enough attention to the challenge of effectively onboarding the new hires to maximize their productivity as quickly as possible.

Ignoring this risk could seriously delay implementation of the new strategy. If you have a lot of new hires, can you answer these questions:

- Do we know the real costs of failing to onboard new managers and workers as effectively as possible?
- What risks do subpar productivity and increased new-hire attrition pose for our business?
- How do we know our onboarding process adequately reduces the time it takes a new employee to get up to speed?

Dissatisfied Employees

With 70 offices worldwide, Baker & McKenzie is the world's largest law firm by headcount. A few years ago, the firm's leadership made improved profitability a primary strategic objective. In the process of implementation, top management overlooked threats to its strategy posed by the steady increase in turnover among the firm's junior associates in recent years. How would this unplanned attrition affect Baker & McKenzie's profit objectives? It turned out that every dissatisfied young attorney who left cost the firm hundreds of thousands of dollars in training, development, and replacement costs, even if the attorney didn't join a competitor.[3]

To accelerate profitable growth, the firm had to better understand and manage the costs of unplanned turnover. To diagnose this risk factor, you need to be able to answer the following questions:

- What are the actual turnover rates for all critical roles or job families in our organization? Are these turnover rates trending in the right direction?
- Even if attrition declined during the last recession, what assumptions are we making about how changes in the economy, retirement eligibility, an improving stock market, and increased employment opportunities will affect unplanned attrition in key parts of our business?

Shortage of Talent in Leadership Pipeline

The new CEO of New York Life, the largest mutual life insurance company in the United States, faced multiple challenges when he looked at his leadership pipeline. Changes in the competitive environment meant future leaders needed new, more entrepreneurial decision-making skills. In addition, 50 percent of the company's top 300 executives would be eligible to retire within five years, and the majority of those roles did not have successors with the right skills to step in. With all these changes, the chief executive knew he had to make reducing the risks of succession planning one of his top priorities.

"Succession risk" is one type of talent-related threat already widely recognized by many risk managers. But that doesn't mean leaders pay enough attention to reducing its potential negative impacts. While many organizations have the trappings of succession planning in place, if you look under the covers, as the CEO at New York Life did, you often will find that, in practice, potential successors are double counted, as if they could fill multiple jobs, and the amount of meaningful mentoring and leadership development actually taking place is limited. This situation means that many firms are making themselves incredibly vulnerable to gaps in their leadership pipelines. To diagnose this risk factor, you need to be able to answer questions such as these:

- Do we have an age profile of our leadership team and our workforce, so we know *specifically* where retirements are likely to come in the near future?
- Do we have historical data on retirement patterns that would allow us to predict when individuals will leave?
- Is our performance management process robust enough to provide effective evaluations of all leaders, including

those veterans who decide to continue working after they are retirement eligible?

- Which hard-to-fill leadership roles most often experience midcareer turnover?[4]

Loss of Critical Skilled Employees

The chief executive of a power generating plant with nearly 4,000 employees faced a different kind of succession risk when he took over recently. He inherited a highly specialized workforce with more than 40 percent of the engineering staff and up to 70 percent of supervisors eligible to retire within five years. To ensure safe operation of the plant in the future, the executive needed to mitigate the risks of critical knowledge loss with so many veterans leaving. This meant he needed to know which employees and supervisors had knowledge and capabilities essential to improving performance and which would not be missed.

In such a situation, you need to be able to adequately and effectively address the following questions:

- Given our future strategy, what critical capabilities are most at risk in our organization?
- How is our firm determining which individuals have unique knowledge essential to the future of the business?
- What will be the costs to the business if these risks go unaddressed?

These talent-related risk factors are among the most common—and most costly if they are ignored. But there are others you will want to explore with your leadership team. Here are a few more examples:

- **Competitors poaching key employees.** A major Midwest bank continued to invest aggressively in leadership development throughout the last recession. As business improved, top management worried that it would become a major recruiting target for other banks that had lost critical talent during the downturn.
- **Key talent geographically dispersed.** The senior manager of a software development department specializing in speech recognition lamented that he had more than 300 employees spread between three continents and six time zones. He found this increased the likelihood of rework, quality problems, and missed deadlines.
- **Generational conflict.** A federal government agency had begun hiring a lot of Millennials to replace retiring older workers. A change in personnel policies meant new hires with a college degree automatically started at a higher pay grade in the civil service system that had taken older baby boomers without college degrees years to achieve. While the younger workers could readily learn the technical aspects of the job, their effectiveness was at risk because veterans who resented the new hiring policies refused to share their critical experiential knowledge with their junior colleagues. Leaders had to find a way to manage this intergenerational conflict to accelerate knowledge transfer.
- **Cost and quality of living.** An aerospace company in Southern California has trouble retaining midcareer engineers who find the region's housing costs untenable when they settle down to raise a family. The CEO of a rural hospital in New Mexico finds his organization has to provide housing in order to recruit allied health pro-

fessionals. Geographic location can have a tremendous impact on a firm's ability to recruit and retain skilled talent.

How to Think About Talent-Related Risk Management

Risk is a concept used loosely in organizations today. Managers talk broadly about security risks, supply chain risks, reputational risks, operational risks, and so on. Many risk discussions are centered on quantitative issues, but the conversations can be confusing because the term is like a Rorschach inkblot test: everybody in the room has a slightly different idea of what is meant by "risk."

Managers also have different ideas about the definition of risk management. For your organization, more or less formality may be appropriate. Even though a growing number of organizations have elaborate risk management processes, the most sophisticated approaches still can produce poor results. Take Merrill Lynch, for example. According to one investment banker, the brokerage firm had 70 pages describing its extensive risk management processes in its last 10-K filing— just before it collapsed and had to be rescued by Bank of America. Having processes for managing risk is one thing, but executing them effectively is what counts.

Unfortunately it is very difficult to prove that most of the risk analysis methods being used in organizations today actually identify the most serious risks and mitigate their effects. Risk experts like Douglas Hubbard make this argument:

The biggest failure of risk management is that there is almost no experimentally verifiable evidence that the methods used improve on the assessment and mitigation of risks, especially for the softer (and much more popular) methods. If the only "evidence" is a subjective perception of success by the very managers who championed the method in the first place, then we have no reason to believe that the risk management method does not have a negative return.[5]

There is, however, a difference between evaluating risk management programs overall and the handling of a specific risk or set of risks. Evaluating the effectiveness of organization-wide risk programs is beyond the scope of this book. We are focused on identifying, prioritizing, and addressing specific risks where cause and effect are relatively obvious. In such cases, the probability of an event and its severity can be reasonably estimated. In addition, it is clear that the risk analysis we are advocating identifies what would be major problems if left unaddressed. An example would be failing to plan for the succession of a strategically critical executive or technical expert. In situations like this, it is safe to conclude that without methodical risk analysis the threat was unlikely to have been highlighted or addressed. In the reverse scenario, there are many examples of costly events that could have been avoided if effective risk management processes were in place.[6]

Despite the limitations, many organizations are already doing a passable job of risk analysis when using more quantifiable methods for traditional management activities in areas such as:

- **Production scheduling.** What are the bottlenecks most likely to threaten our production goals?
- **Operations management.** What materials in our supply chain come from a single supplier?

- **Financial planning.** What are the chances we won't have adequate cash flow to meet production costs?
- **Legal planning.** How do we structure this partnership to avoid litigation later?

Few executive teams, however, approach their talent risks with this same rigor. Do you share status, review proposals, and troubleshoot problems related to hiring, training, and development? Are you regularly reviewing problem areas like these?

- **Headcount planning.** Which positions (e.g., senior project managers) or skills (e.g., product design) may be in short supply?
- **Recruiting.** Who are we competing with for critical new hires? What keeps good candidates from accepting our job offers?
- **Leadership development.** What will happen if we don't have enough leaders in the pipeline to manage all this work?
- **Training and development (formal and informal).** Will our employees have the right skills? What if they can't adjust when we need to change quickly?
- **Human resources systems.** Does our compensation and benefits package support our retention needs?

Depending upon your organization's approach, you may view talent management risks in the context of a broad enterprise risk management process, or you may analyze these threats on the back of a napkin with your management team. However formal or informal your process, these three principles will help you work with colleagues who are likely to have different perspectives on risk management: (1) industries differ in their perceptions of talent risks; (2) perspectives on risk can vary significantly, depending on your role; and (3) risk assessments may be subjective.

First, industries and organizations view talent-related risks differently. For example, the banking industry has been in a period of consolidation for so long that layoffs at all levels have become a way of life. Thus, it may be harder to get banking executives to think seriously about recruiting and succession risks. On the other hand, the utilities industry has been worrying about an aging workforce for years now, so the need to confront attrition risk has become more accepted. In comparison, leaders in the R&D group of a major high-tech firm refuse to think in terms of risks when it comes to managing talent. They view recruiting only in positive terms: as an opportunity to hire the best experts in the world. For this firm, not having people available to execute the strategy is not the risk; hiring the wrong people is the risk. One VP of R&D said, "I want to bring in the best people, so I don't think of coming up short in recruiting as a risk to the business because that would encourage me to go after some expert just to fill a hole."

As these examples show, an important risk for one industry may not be that important to another. Look at your own industry's recent history to surface potential blind spots you might have developed in evaluating risks. For example, just because layoffs have been the norm in recent years doesn't mean recruiting risks for certain critical roles are not a real threat to sustaining growth.

Second, people perceive talent-related risks very differently, depending on their role, experience level, and time horizon.[7]

The CEO worried about developing leaders who will be ready to take senior positions in five years is going to view succession risks differently than a functional vice president anxious to retain a high flier who is helping the unit meet performance goals today. Expect your colleagues, particularly those in other functions and business units, to have different perspectives on the organization's most critical talent risks. If you need the support of other executives to mitigate particular risks, then build in time for discussions needed to reach agreement on which threats are the real priorities.

Third, discussions about talent risks are difficult because there is no widely shared language or tools for reconciling different views of these risks and how to manage them. The many quantitative tools for assessing risk have helped create distinct domains of risk expertise that seldom interact: for example, actuaries, financial analysts, and economists.[8] But identifying the probabilities and potential negative outcomes related to talent has primarily relied on more subjective assessments, using methods such as expert intuition, risk matrices, and weighted scores.

Risk experts like Douglas Hubbard have taken to skewering these subjective approaches to risk analysis as "worse than useless," in part, because they breed overconfidence on the part of executives who may believe they are addressing their most critical risks and that their mitigation efforts are having the desired effects.[9] We will address the payoff of talent management solutions in Chapter 8.

But in terms of identifying and prioritizing the most serious talent-related risks, you have several options. First, if you want to stop your talent managers in their tracks, ask them these questions:

- How do you know this risk analysis method works?
- In terms of risk management, how do we define success?
- What will be the consequences if our approach for assessing talent-related risks doesn't work (e.g., wasted time and resources, overlooked threats)?[10]

In all likelihood, proponents of more subjective approaches to risk management will only be able to demonstrate that they are using "weakly effective methods." That is, participants like using the method and they are satisfied with the outcomes of the analysis. But there was no demonstrated impact on business outcomes.[11]

Second, as Hubbard suggests, you can advocate for more quantitative and validated approaches, which may or may not be realistic, given your resources and the specific issues you are addressing.[12] Or, finally, you could continue to use one of the subjective methods that have become so popular, such as the risk matrix described in the next section, fully aware of its limitations. These tools can be good for surfacing otherwise overlooked talent-related risks and for developing a shared understanding of what risks leaders judge to be most important. But that's the limit of what they can do. Any claims of their additional value, such as valid ranking of risks, must be judged skeptically.

Identifying Talent-Related Threats: Three Levels of Risk Analysis

Three levels of risk analysis are needed when addressing talent-related threats: strategic risks, tactical risks, and operational risks (otherwise known as emergencies).

Identifying Strategic Risk Factors

Of course it depends on your role in the organization, but as a rule you should start with a high-level strategic risk analysis and then drill down to diagnose specific risks and potential mitigation strategies. At the highest level, a common risk analysis tool is the two-by-two matrix shown in Figure 4.1.

Here's how leaders in one health-care organization used this matrix to identify and prioritize risks. In a daylong retreat, the executive team started broadly by continually asking, "What are the biggest risks that could impede us from achieving our overall business strategy?" As risks surfaced, such as increased medical malpractice costs, the group scored each threat both in terms of likelihood of occurring (1 = low to 5 = very high) and potential damage to the organization's performance (1 = low to 5 = severe). Obviously, those risks

FIGURE 4.1   Two-by-Two Risk Analysis Matrix

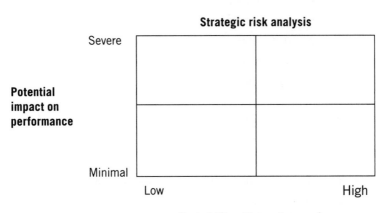

that scored 25 or 20, when the two dimensions were multiplied, needed the most attention.

Hospital executives went further by asking, "What are we already doing to mitigate this particular risk? And what else should we be doing to reduce its impact or probability of occurring?" Finally, participants also asked, "If we're successful at taking those additional risk mitigation steps, how much will we affect the potential damage of that risk?" Then they rescored the risk under discussion, sometimes finding they could reduce a risk score from 25 to 15 by reducing its likelihood of occurring.

The hospital's president noted, "After going through this organization-wide risk assessment process, we were surprised to find that the top-rated risks were not how to deal with things like national health-care reform. The biggest issues that showed the vulnerability of achieving our strategy were tied to effective leadership development."

Drilling Down to Clarify Tactical Threats

For some leaders, this strategic level of risk analysis will be enough. But many executives will need to drill down further into risk factors to identify specifically where the most serious threats to organizational performance are located. In an ideal world, executives would be able to state their workforce needs in the most pragmatic terms. For example:

- (Number of units) of work required to meet (number of units) of customer demand will require (number of units) of skilled workers.
- For example, 60 man-hours of work required to assemble 100 blenders per day requires 8.7 FTE fully capable of assembling the ACME 2000 blender.

Managing risk would be a lot easier if every position in a global workforce could be as clear as this. The trouble is that what it means to be "fully capable" in many jobs today is unclear, and this lack of clarity creates all kinds of problems when analyzing risk. Plenty of consultants can explain how to ensure that a manufacturing employee is fully capable of assembling a blender, but many jobs are not so straightforward. How can senior leaders assess and mitigate risks when asked to approve the following request?

> *The schedule says it will take six months to write the code for the new software module explained in the specification. It looks like we'll need about 20 smart developers to get it done.*

If all "smart developers" were equally capable, this formula might be good enough, but that isn't the case. Twenty developers might be available, but the risk comes in knowing little about their individual and collective capacity to get the job done. Who in his or her right mind would risk the success of a business on such a vague proposition? In fact, it happens every day.

Headcount Plans, Demographic Profiles, and Competency Models Aren't Enough

Here's how many leaders approach talent planning today. They have access to a "headcount plan" that lists employees by function or job title. If pressed, they can produce a report that shows, for example, how many engineers, marketers, or assembly technicians they have right now, and they can probably explain their decision process for how many will be in the budget for next year. This process of adding or removing headcount in the plan worked reasonably well for decades when the workforce was relatively stable and a steady stream of talent was standing by. Risk management primarily consisted of not hiring too many, or not having too few employees in case production needed to be increased quickly.

A growing number of organizations today have gone to the trouble of developing age profiles of their workforce.[13] This allows them to analyze trends, such as who is likely to retire soon, or to review turnover numbers for younger workers. Many organizations have also developed "competency models" that list vague abilities like "communicator," "problem solver," or "project manager." While competency models have proved valuable in some situations, often those vague categories are of limited use in analyzing a workforce or leadership pipeline.

With the changes in workforce demographics, and with more turnover among younger employees, headcount plans, age profiles, and competency models are no longer sufficient as a solution to ensuring a ready workforce. In the past, some assumptions about an employee's abilities could be made based on his or her résumé, job classification, and tenure: "If he did that, he can probably handle this."

There are two problems with this approach. Work is increasingly complex, fluid, and changing, and employees are much less likely to stay in one place long enough for their capabilities and potential to be well known by management. The crew that has worked together for 10-plus years under the same supervisor doing the same type of work has become a thing of the past.

Today, working from generic job descriptions and headcount plans creates too great a risk that the people plugged into those positions will not be fully capable of doing the job.

Executives can no longer approve hiring 50 "software testers" in Bangalore without knowing in some detail what work they will be doing. The likelihood of failure—and the cost of it—is too high.

Is Your Talent Risk Assessment Specific Enough?

Whether onboarding new employees or cross-training veteran workers already on the payroll, executives need a more transparent way to deploy and redeploy their workforce in a quick and nimble fashion—pointing the right employees at the work and knowing that the risk of failure is reasonably low. They also need to be able to see two or three years into the future and know where their specific talent risks lie. If an accounting firm such as Deloitte needs CPAs, and it takes five years to develop one, Deloitte can't start its talent planning with this year's crop of graduates.

If a high-tech firm's strategy suggests moving away from hardware development and into more software development, hiring executives should not simply be approving requests for "software developers."

The EVP of auditing for a major bank explained her talent risk assessment problem this way:

> *If I don't have the right talent who understands the bank's products and processes, then I'm at risk of not finding a gap in the control processes that would later manifest as a big problem. So these skill risks can translate into financial and reputational risks. And without a structured skills assessment process, I wouldn't know where the gaps are. Our HR department doesn't have a framework for doing this. They want to stay at the competencies level, but I've told them we need to go deeper than that.*

As these examples show, lack of clarity creates risk. Leaders must have a framework to articulate and communicate the specific skills they need to execute their strategy, and that framework must be simple to use and maintain. We developed a tool that fits these criteria that has been used effectively in a variety of industries: the Knowledge Silo Matrix (KSM).

Knowledge Silo Matrix: A Framework for Risk Assessment
The KSM not only makes current workforce readiness explicit, but also, when compared against skills needed for the future, enables effective risk analysis by making emerging skill gaps obvious. A silo is a specific knowledge domain, and the Knowledge Silo Matrix identifies each employee's level of knowledge in each domain. (See Figure 4.2.)

As a framework, the KSM can help:

- Identify and list the "silos of knowledge," such as tools, processes, platforms, standards, products, customers, and history, that exist within an organization (top row on the matrix in Figure 4.2).
- Count the individuals who have specific expertise and who are capable of doing the work associated with that silo.
- Identify individuals who would be appropriate "peer mentors" not only because they are capable of doing the work but also because their approach sets the standard for others.
- Call out individuals to learn specific silos, designated here as "apprentices."
- Highlight clear risks to the business unit in getting the job done.

FIGURE 4.2 Knowledge Silo Matrix

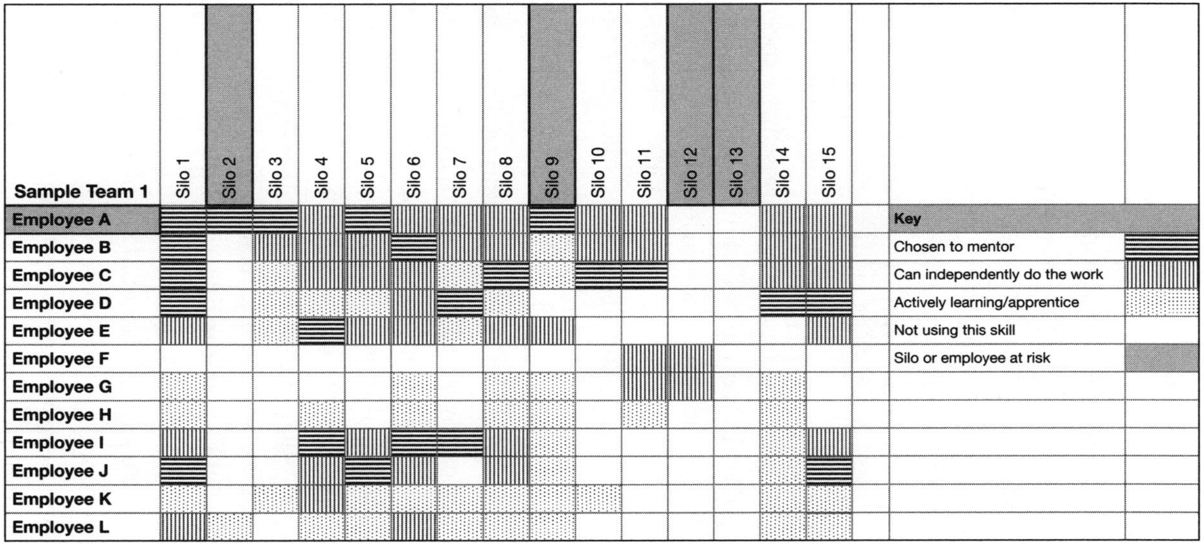

Key

	Chosen to mentor
	Can independently do the work
	Actively learning/apprentice
	Not using this skill
	Silo or employee at risk

(Silos are specific knowledge domains)

Silo 2 is at risk because in the near future the team will need six skilled people and currently has only one.

Silo 9 is at risk because so many people are trying to learn from one mentor.

Silo 12 is at risk because neither of the employees skilled in that area is good enough to mentor.

Silo 13 is at risk because the only skilled person recently left the group (no one marked on the silo at all).

Employee A is at risk because too much of the team's success is dependent on him or her being asked to mentor in too many silos.

Here's how one organization used the KSM to clarify and prioritize the risks posed by the expected retirement of critical skilled employees.

The director of engineering at a major power generating station had only been on the job for several months when he had to clarify serious risks related to his future workforce. With 40 percent of the engineers in his unit nearing retirement, the director knew that the pending loss of expertise had serious productivity, safety, and morale implications for the organization. Like other power plants, this facility is highly regulated by the government. Recent audits had cited workforce training as a serious concern and raised the specter of the site being put on probation, which was only one step from being shut down, a disastrous scenario for the company. In addition, the director knew he had to act fast because the economy was improving and he expected the rate of retirement among his senior engineers to accelerate.

The director assumed that his aging engineering workforce was the primary risk he had to address. But with 350 full-time employees covering dozens of areas of expertise, he had no idea where the greatest threats lay in terms of losing critical skills and capabilities. For example, he had to make sure trained replacements could sustain safe operations in specialized areas such as fire protection, security systems, heating and cooling, and plant safety. To identify the specific capabilities most at risk, the engineering director chose to use the Knowledge Silo Matrix. In developing a KSM, his team created an inventory of all essential deep and narrow areas of expertise covered by the engineering division. The 350 knowledge domains, or silos, identified in discussions with managers and employee interviews, were arrayed in columns across the horizontal dimension of the matrix (see Figure 4.2).

The team then listed on the vertical dimension all employees in the organization whose job responsibilities required some mastery of any of the knowledge silos.

By surveying supervisors, senior staff rated each employee in terms of capabilities in relevant knowledge domains. In Figure 4.2, these codes appear in black and white, but his version used colors to make the problem areas even more visible. Engineers were scored on the matrix as:

- **"Expert/chosen to mentor"** (shown as dark horizontal lines in the matrix). These employees were called out as the "standard bearers" for the silo of knowledge. This meant they were doing the work in the way their managers wanted to replicate in others. (They might also have shown an aptitude for mentoring, but that was considered secondary.) It wasn't enough for these employees to be "the best we've got." It was better to note that no one was available as a mentor and to deal with that challenge, instead of planning to replicate the skills of someone who wasn't going to train others at a level that sustained quality performance.
- **"Can independently do the work"** (vertical lines). These engineers were thought to be "solid citizens," who get their work done every day without extensive support from others. Most employees fall into this category, which is fine. Those designated in this category may be there because the manager doesn't want or need them to mentor others for a variety of reasons. Organizations need plenty of dependable workers.
- **"Actively learning/apprentice"** (dots). These employees were the "apprentices" who were assigned by their managers to learn from mentors. Being identified as "actively

learning" meant more than general job shadowing. It meant that a plan for methodical knowledge transfer had been designed, and there were specific expectations for the employee to develop the skills in that particular silo.

Cells were left blank if individual employees were not doing work that required knowledge in a particular silo. In addition to categorizing levels of employee knowledge, each silo was analyzed to determine associated risks using criteria, such as mission criticality, current on-site expertise, time to expected retirement, difficulty in hiring expertise from outside the company, and overall skill complexity, which affected ramp-up time. Silos were ranked by degree of risk on a five-point scale, 1 being highest risk. Silos most at risk were shaded red (shown with heavier shading in Figure 4.2). (For a more detailed sample of a KSM in color see our website, http://www .HighImpactTalentManagement.com.)

Using the KSM to Analyze Risk

Creating a visual display showing the distribution and depth of engineering's expertise gave the director and his team a much clearer understanding of the immediate and longer-term risks they faced due to potential loss of skills in specific domains. For example, in conversations with his managers, the engineering director could review the status of his 32 teams to clarify priorities and options. He asked the following series of questions:

- **How many workers need to be skilled in each silo two to five years from now, and how many do we have now (gap analysis)?** The director and his managers could now review each silo and consider the likely volume of work in the medium to long term. Some silos were already becoming obsolete, and it would be okay to let that experience go away. But others were going to ramp up in volume or were critical enough to require fully capable backups at all times. Now, instead of saying, "We're probably going to need more systems engineers next year." They could use the KSM and say, "We'll need to have four engineers able to support the plant fire protection system next year, and it looks like we're probably going to be at least two short."

- **What is the demographic profile of each employee noted as "expert/mentor"?** (Note: Risk is not reduced by youth, it is only heightened by age.) The director's team overlaid the expected date of retirement for each employee on top of the data from the KSM to further enhance the risk profile. He found one team of systems engineers all over 60 years old, while other teams had a majority of very young engineers. The engineering director was able to use the information in the Knowledge Silo Matrix, along with the demographic profiles, to reorganize and balance the teams in terms of experience. In the process, he recognized a misguided assumption under which his managers had been working. As they reviewed the KSM, they found a number of engineers with unique knowledge. That is, each of these engineers was *the only employee* identified as an expert/mentor or as working independently in a specific silo. In cases where a lone engineer with unique knowledge was *not* also nearing retirement, managers consistently deemed the risk low and moved on to other silos. They were working on the assumption that a younger engineer was not at risk because, for years, most employees would join the plant and stay their whole careers. That is no longer a safe assumption, and the director of engineering began using the KSM results to push for "apprentices" in every critical silo where there was no backup—regardless of the age of the current expert.

- **What if there is no expert/mentor in a specific department? Can mentors be shared?** (If not, the risk would be higher.) On several teams the supervisors might have one or two employees able to perform tasks adequately, but there was no one who could be called a "standard bearer" and in a position to cross-train others. In these cases, the KSM database was mined for silo mentors in other departments who could be drafted to cross-train outside their immediate teams. Thus, the director and his senior managers could use the best mentors for each silo to help the larger organization improve consistency and quality.

- **How readily available in the marketplace are the skills in this silo?** Once the director and his managers used the KSM to identify the highest risk silos, they considered ways to reduce the risks of not having enough trained employees for each one. In some cases, it was just a matter of cross-training within an existing team. In other cases, though, such as for some of the plant's systems engineers, they had to try to hire the expertise. One key issue then was how readily they would be able to find this talent on the market. They could now articulate this question more clearly to their recruiting team because they had very specific capability needs identified.

- **How long does it take to bring an inexperienced new employee up to speed?** Another key benefit of the risk analysis process was identifying how long it would take to make a new or transferred employee productive in each silo. Some skill areas were routine and could be mastered in weeks; other silos were complex enough to require months, or even years, of on-the-job training. Engineering's senior leadership team asked for a detailed skill/task analysis of the most complex silos as a way to more carefully determine how much lead time would be needed to provide backups for the highest risk silos.

- **What are the costs of bringing someone up to speed in this silo over time versus in a time crunch?** As the team reviewed the most critical silos, they knew that lack of planning increased time pressures and could increase both their risk of failure and the costs associated with transferring essential skills. For example, one engineer left the company on short notice and with no backup. The only way to replace his skills quickly was to hire an expensive consultant to come in and do the work. This was a strain on the budget and not a long-term solution. The team still had to hire and train a replacement with only a consultant to serve as the mentor.

- **What are the remedies for a shortage of the skills in a particular silo?** With a clearer picture of his risks, the director could request a full inventory of the talent management resources available to hire, train, or cross-train and manage the development of a fully capable workforce.

As he looked at the silos of knowledge across his organization, the director could see what skill sets were used in each department. And by slicing the data another way, he could see what levels of experience existed elsewhere for each silo. If necessary, he could also look at the skill profile of each employee to make decisions about where each would be best deployed. In the end, the director could now be very clear when communicating priorities to his talent management team. He could ask, "What can you do to fill *this* critical silo in my KSM with sufficient talent to meet the workload?"

Spotting High-Stakes Operational Risks

Sometimes threats to business performance due to talent risks are emergencies and require quick recognition and action to minimize negative impacts and to maximize business opportunities.

For example, one fast-growing pharmaceutical company was faced with hiring more than 300 salespeople in just a few weeks to support a new product launch in its largest market. Management estimated that every day they didn't have a qualified salesperson calling on physicians the company was losing $50,000 in revenues, so there was tremendous pressure to hire new staff and get them in the field. But there was also a bigger risk that hiring too quickly would result in more costly bad hires. Management estimated that hiring more than 300 salespeople in a month would result in one in four being a bad hire, which was very costly. Working with the recruiting staff, leaders had to decide how to hire quickly enough to maximize revenues effectively while minimizing the costs of too many bad hires. In the end, management decided to hire in phases, taking on 225 salespeople in the first month to support the product launch, which reduced the pressure on hiring managers that could result in bad choices.

Another talent-related operational risk is the loss of key employees who receive job offers from other firms. How executives respond when a valuable employee announces he or she is resigning to take another position has a major impact on whether or not the person actually leaves. Of course, often nothing can be done to change an employee's mind, but systems and tactics have been developed to combat this situation. For example, T. J. Rodgers, CEO of Cypress Semiconductor Corporation, has developed an eight-step system for responding to these threats, which can reverse the decision of about half of those planning to leave.[14] Here are four of the main steps in Rodgers' strategy for retaining key employees who have announced they are resigning:

1. **React immediately** (within five minutes). Leaders must demonstrate that keeping a good colleague takes precedence over everything at that moment.
2. **Keep the resignation a secret.** This makes it much more likely the employee can change his or her mind without losing face or appearing to vacillate on a critical decision.
3. **Tell your boss immediately.** There is no excuse for not informing every executive in the chain of command up to the CEO within the hour about a critical resignation. Giving key leaders time to respond is critical to possibly reversing the decision.
4. **Listen carefully to the employee.** The individual's manager and the manager's boss should immediately sit down with the person resigning and listen intently to understand the exact reasons why the person is leav-

ing. Top management can't respond effectively unless the executives know precisely what is motivating the employee to go. "I don't like working for you" is one response management must be able to hear and respond to with constructive options (e.g., reassignment) if there is any chance to reverse the decision.[15]

Retirements that create a serious loss of critical knowledge are another operational risk that can have an immediate negative impact on organizational performance. A technician making control boards on a radar equipment assembly line at Texas Instruments retired; immediately, parts coming off the line began failing quality assurance tests. Engineering consultants couldn't find the problem, which forced a shutdown of the assembly line and cost the unit more than $200,000 in lost sales revenues, before the retired technician was brought back to identify and fix the problem.[16] Often, executives wait too long to recognize the risk of critical knowledge loss, making formal transfer processes impractical. In this case, the only options are usually to outsource the activities or to rehire the retiree as a contractor to sustain the capability.

Talent-related operational risks have a different quality than strategic and tactical risks. They are emergencies. They exist in specific situations where there is a high probability of serious negative impact on performance. There is little time to act, but timely executive decisions can make a big difference. There are three things you can do to more effectively identify operational risks:

1. Recognize the types of risks that can arise unexpectedly and unnoticed by others. The sooner you identify a pos-

sible threat to performance, the more time you have to react.

2. Think explicitly about the potential costs to the business of not addressing this threat.

3. Ask what steps you could take to mitigate this immediate threat. Often you have more options than you realize when trying to talk a key employee out of resigning, creating productive assignments for high potentials, or minimizing the costs of lost knowledge. The sooner you identify and act on these options the more likely you are to limit the damage, and even turn the situation into an opportunity for improved performance. But always consider the new risks you might be creating by taking a particular action. For example, the CEO at Cypress could create unintended compensation issues if he responded too generously to an employee threatening to leave for another firm.

Part of diagnosing and prioritizing risks is knowing the limitations and pitfalls of the methods you are using. It is also knowing the resources you currently have in place to address your most critical risks. The threat of having a dangerously thin leadership pipeline, for example, may be less serious if you know for certain that you have an elaborate set of programs already in place to recruit and accelerate the development of future leaders. But how should you evaluate these talent-related initiatives? In other words, how do you accurately assess the current state of your talent management efforts? That's the focus of Chapter 5.

For Talent Management and HR Business Partners

Make Explicit the Goals of Talent Management

HR innovators can use this chapter to talk about talent risks with senior executives. As business partners, HR leaders should describe these risks using the language of the business.

How are you currently communicating risk to your line executives? If you're like most HR professionals, you're probably using a mix of competency models and demographic data. Line executives, however, are often unimpressed and annoyed by the relatively vague language of competency models and the relatively faceless data associated with workforce demographics. Instead, they want more specific information about the dangers of not having the workforce and leadership team they will need in 24 to 36 months.

Using the tools described here, you can frame talent risks in practical terms. For example, in the Knowledge Silo Matrix (Figure 4.2), the knowledge silos describe the technical knowledge domains using the everyday language of the business. That means an engineer is called out as the "mentor for elastic fracture mechanics," not the competency model's overly vague "drives for results." The sales team is defined by people who can "negotiate C-level contracts," not the competency model's platitude, "focus on the customer."

Using the Knowledge Silo Matrix, you can define the "capability gap," examine shortfalls in specific required capabilities, and assess bench strength. To get a sense of how the Knowledge Silo Matrix helps you see potential talent risks, start by making a Knowledge Silo Matrix for your own team. What do you learn about the capabilities required for your group? In what areas are you dependent on a single individual? How would the mix of skills represented by your team members change if key people left?

Next, sit with a trusted colleague in the business unit and work at a first draft of the Knowledge Silo Matrix for a small group in the unit itself. Take on one team where you can build a Knowledge Silo Matrix and start to show the capability gap just for that team. Even at this pilot level, you'll uncover bottlenecks, discover pending capability shortages, and get a better understanding of dependencies on individual employees. You can use this data in the next round of hiring or to spotlight a need for more formal training. By working through a specific example in detail, you show your business partners the value of talking about capabilities gaps on a broader scale. Then, when you look at a complete list of knowledge silos, you can lead a discussion about priorities, as described in this chapter. For more detailed examples of Knowledge Silo Matrices in color, see http://www.HighImpactTalentManage ment.com.

When you give the line executive a baseline measure of skills and knowledge, you help make explicit the goals of talent management programs. Setting out the risks gives your business executive the information necessary to decide whether or not to spend time and other resources on talent management—as well as to justify these expenditures to more senior leaders and other stakeholders.

You become a business partner only by describing risks and outlining solutions in terms that affect business results. When you give your business executive a clear statement of risk, that leader—armed with data—can then create, champion, and implement the talent management solutions you offer.

5

Evaluating Existing Initiatives—
What Role Does Culture Play?

The United Kingdom–based consumer products company mentioned in Chapter 1 couldn't grow because its highly praised succession planning process was inadequate. The public utility described in Chapter 2 had more than two dozen consultants on site—each working on a different, uncoordinated piece of workforce and leadership development. In both of these instances, executives didn't have a clear idea of what was actually going on with talent management. This opacity makes it impossible to perform an essential executive function: evaluating existing initiatives to identify which investments should be expanded, fixed, nixed, or reinvented.

This chapter shows how to assess talent management initiatives, starting with a straightforward inventory of programs, which positions you to understand how your existing culture supports or undermines objectives for creating a ready workforce and leadership team. To diagnose the current state of talent management in your organization, you must also understand current practices, behavioral norms, stated values (even if they conflict with actual behaviors!), and shared but unspoken assumptions. This chapter gives you a simple way to make explicit these components of your corporate culture. This is important for two reasons. First, it will help explain why some current initiatives are succeeding, while others don't seem to have any impact. Second, taking culture into account will help you make more effective decisions about what talent management and leadership development solutions will work best going forward.

Types of Talent Management Inventories and Assessments

Executives are called upon to evaluate existing talent management initiatives on three different levels: First, you might want to take a comprehensive look at all existing talent-related investments in your corporation or division. Second, you may need to identify and evaluate ongoing initiatives related to particular problem areas like succession planning or mentoring. Third, your focus may be assessing a specific initiative, such as, "What's the impact of the knowledge transfer program in our R&D department where key scientists are retiring next year?"

The inability to effectively assess talent initiatives on these three levels has serious costs that include the following:

1. Redundant talent management programs due to poor communication and coordination
2. Resources wasted attempting to solve the wrong problem because of a failure to link to clear business needs
3. Lack of institutional memory that leads to repeated ineffective attempts to solve the same problem
4. Continued showcasing and investment in programs that get lots of publicity but actually produce minimal results

5. Successful programs cancelled by new leaders who prefer to make their marks with a new effort
6. Partially solving problems in reaction to a crisis, instead of proactively planning and prioritizing talent management needs

Making a Comprehensive Inventory Useful

A surprising number of organizations fail to look at their talent management programs as a whole. As a result, these efforts evolve in a helter-skelter fashion. You want a new mentoring program? Fine. We need an initiative to retain high potentials? Okay. We're hiring 50 new people into a group of only 100? Uh-oh, better whip up an onboarding program.

Remember, we've defined talent management as "all efforts related to delivering the workforce and leadership capabilities needed to execute on the business strategy." This definition encompasses a wide range of possible activities within the three broad areas of talent acquisition, talent development, and talent retention. Many activities, programs, and processes support talent management (see Table 5.1 on page 109), and it can be difficult to keep track of them all. A simple list is a surprisingly powerful way to improve the effectiveness and efficiency of your overall investment in talent management.

Benefits of an inventory include the following:

• Helps managers communicate priorities when talent management activities conflict with each other or with other work priorities
• Helps identify programs serving a small group of people that could easily be extended to other parts of the organization

- Creates institutional memory by recording what has been done over time, by whom, and why, so people are not continually trying to solve the same problem
- Helps managers overseeing different talent management programs communicate, share information, and identify economies of scale
- Reveals programs that are redundant or underutilized
- Makes it possible to discuss the results of each activity because programs appear on the list relative to others and are more likely to be compared
- Encourages evaluation of how a proposed program fits with existing investments before it is implemented
- Establishes an important ground rule that a coordinated approach to talent management is expected

Creating a Comprehensive Inventory

When requesting an inventory, ask what practices, programs, and processes you have in place to address both immediate and future talent needs. Be clear about the level of detail you'd like. Set some ground rules about the cost and importance of the programs you want to review. Some talent management activities (e.g., a formal succession plan) would certainly make your list; others (e.g., informal networking lunches) may or may not.

Think of the inventory as an informal snapshot, and make clear to your team that you're not looking for a three-week study with project management time lines and formal presentations. State explicitly how much time this should take and what you want to see. For example, in a large organization, the charge might be, "Please spend up to five hours, and bring me a list no longer than two pages."

TABLE 5.1   Sample of Talent Management–Related Practices, Initiatives, Processes, and Systems

Talent Acquisition	Talent Development	Talent Retention	General
• Recruiting • Onboarding • Outsourcing • Intern programs	• Training • Peer mentoring • Communities of practice • Career development • Performance management • Social networking and Web 2.0 applications • Leadership development • Succession planning • Management development • High-potential talent pools • Career mentoring • Lessons learned databases	• High potentials program • Rotational programs • Career counseling • Diversity programs • Affinity groups • Retraining • Phased retirement	• Engagement or high-performance culture • Information technology infrastructure

Here are some criteria you might want to use to decide whether or not to include an initiative in the inventory:

- Affects or helps a significant number (specify relevant number) of people as participants (e.g., candidates recruited, students trained, leader successions planned, etc.)

- Targets employees or managers from key groups (e.g., job category, level, tenure, location, etc.)
- Planning and execution involves a significant number of employees and/or person-hours
- Spans an unusual period of days or months
- Transcends key organizational boundaries or silos (e.g., across teams, departments, or locations, or is visible to customers)
- Costs more than X dollars or euros

Analyzing the Inventory

Once you get some basic information on talent management activities, you can dive into the details until you are satisfied that the program is going to help develop a ready workforce and leadership team. Some of the more obvious questions you might ask include the following:

- Who is targeted with the program (e.g., new hires, a specific job function, or specific team)?
- What are the goals of the initiative? What problem is it solving?
- Who is the internal customer for the program (e.g., an executive sponsor or a specific line manager)?
- Who paid for the program (if it had direct costs), or who would have paid for it (if it did not have direct costs, but used internal resources)?
- What is the timing?
- What does it cost (employees' time plus external help)?
- How are the results tracked or measured?

Some of the less obvious questions could include:

- What is the history of this effort? If it failed in the past, why?
- What else is going on that is either parallel to or in conflict with this solution?
- What alternatives were considered?
- What are or would be the consequences of doing nothing?
- How does this talent management effort map to the business strategy and the cultural norms?
- Is there an exit strategy for this program, or will it go on indefinitely?
- What are the risks that the effort could fail (such as competing priorities), and what is being done to mitigate those risks?

Insisting on an inventory requires having the courage to ask hard questions that subordinates—and even superiors—should have been asking from the beginning. With a complete talent management inventory in hand, you're in a much better position to (1) make sure individual talent management initiatives are integrated with existing programs; (2) turn around a failing program; and (3) make a case for new—and potentially critical—talent investments.

Problem-Focused Inventories

While a comprehensive inventory is ideal, particularly for new executives in large organizations, as a practical matter you will more likely need to evaluate existing programs in a particular problem area. For example, a software company knew it needed to change the way it brought on and trained new employees to advance its new fast-growth strategy and plan for global expansion. An inventory of activities in onboarding and training revealed several important insights including the following:

- **Inadequate product training for staff.** Employees simply used the company's excellent customer training, which was assumed to be sufficient. But the inventory, which included a careful look at the skills learned, showed that some core skills for technical people were not included in the customer training. This was seriously hurting technical employees' ability to take on more work.
- **New training needed to support the global expansion.** The inventory also showed that no attention had been given to the training required to support the new multinational strategy. For example, training to understand and apply international income tax codes was now needed.
- **Inconsistent onboarding and training for new employees.** Historically, this software company had been slow growing, without many new employees. New people came on intermittently in ad hoc fashion, which was fine in the past but not suited to the new high-growth strategy. The inventory made plain the inconsistency in onboarding and supported the need for a program that imparted core information about the company as a whole and structured a new person's transition to a team.
- **Opportunities identified to cross-train.** By examining what was being done in every function, the inventory revealed opportunities to cross-train. For example, con-

sulting services offered a semiannual boot camp. The inventory showed that people from technical services and software development could also benefit from this training.

When evaluating existing programs in a particular problem area, here are three things to watch for:

1. Situations where current initiatives may be misfiring—producing irrelevant or counterproductive results, such as when product training designed for customers was used to train employees
2. Talent programs not keeping up with new business needs dictated by a changing strategy, evolving organization, or competitive environment (The software company's global expansion dictated major changes in training were needed.)
3. Lack of standardized processes that create missed opportunities for improved results in areas such as onboarding and performance management

Evaluating an Existing Program

Sometimes there is no time or need to focus on the larger picture. Instead, you need to evaluate a single existing program. This calls for a different approach. For example, a few months after taking over as chief operating officer for an East Coast utility, the COO suspected that his summer engineering intern program was in trouble. With a high percentage of his engineers expected to retire soon, hiring a lot of young engineers fast was a top priority. Therefore, the COO was concerned about one of the major recruiting programs at the company—internships—and wanted to understand the current process in place. He started by asking, "What are we doing for the engineering interns who have just joined us this summer?"

An HR staffer explained that the interns had received an offer letter for the summer assignment, but nothing else had been done. Indeed, some interns had shown up at the plant without knowing where to park and then had been dumped on engineering teams who weren't expecting them. As a result, the students' experiences were unpredictable at best. A few interns found themselves doing interesting and productive work, while others were doing menial tasks and some were just ignored.

The COO knew this approach was disastrous because disaffected interns could end up not only refusing to return once they graduated, but also discouraging their classmates from applying in the future. His informal questioning had revealed a costly gap in the utility's talent management strategy: not enough was being done to support a major recruiting activity that could have a long-term negative impact on the engineering team if not handled correctly.

This executive began the turnaround of the program by continuing to ask questions such as the following:

- What can we do for the interns who are already here to make sure they have a productive, positive experience?
- Which senior leaders are directly involved as sponsors of this program?
- How are the interns being evaluated? How do they receive feedback?
- What are the criteria for ensuring that interns have challenging projects?

- Once these interns return to school, what are we doing to maintain relationships with those who are potential recruits to ensure the best candidates feel welcome to return?
- What success metrics and follow-up are in place to make sure the program is improved?

When you're looking at an existing talent management program that seems to be in trouble, you can ask questions such as these to ensure that the problem is clear, the target audience for the solution is understood, accountability is in place, and results can be expected.

Evaluating a Proposed Talent Initiative

A proposed program may not yet technically be part of an inventory of talent-related investments, but it isn't uncommon to find programs that are "already in the works" or that have been "approved by your predecessor." Frequently, new leaders arrive and have an opportunity to embrace, change, or eliminate programs that have not been fully implemented. Understanding and evaluating a program that is still being developed is different than assessing an existing initiative. It's easier to change or cancel it. That's why it is important to carefully evaluate the program before making any decisions on how to proceed. Just as it takes courage to cancel a program that's not on strategy, it also takes courage to keep a program you have inherited, instead of killing it and starting over. As much as possible, focus on the value you expect to gain from a program before you consider the added layer of political pressures.

For example, a large power utility expects to lose up to 70 percent of its supervisors in the next few years, so HR approached top management with a proposal for a "leadership academy." This new program would take supervisors away from their desks for five weeks to put them through a leadership boot camp. The utility's new director was uneasy about the proposed program, but she didn't know how to challenge the HR staff on the plans. Here's what she could have asked:

- How does this fit with the other activities or programs we have to address the looming shortage of trained supervisors?
- How did you decide it would take five weeks to conduct this program?
- What alternatives did you consider?
- Who is your customer/sponsor for this leadership academy, and what role is this person playing to ensure it is on target?
- Who is developing the program, and what qualifies them to do a good job?
- How will you measure its success?
- How are you going to backfill the positions of supervisors who will be away for five weeks while they focus on the training?
- How will you choose participants for the program?
- How will you follow the progress of the participants, and what are your contingency plans for people who don't do well in the program?

When you need to do a quick analysis on a proposed initiative, questions like these are a good place to start.

Using Culture to Drive Talent Management

Whether you are developing a comprehensive inventory of talent-related initiatives, evaluating efforts around a particular problem, or assessing a specific program, the organization's culture will always be a major factor in determining success. It doesn't matter if you are evaluating existing or potential investments. Effectively diagnosing and leveraging your culture is probably the most important factor in determining the long-term success of your talent management strategy.

Experienced executives have consistently pointed out to us that "culture trumps strategy." This goes for both business and talent management strategies. You can have the most elegant leadership development plans imaginable, but if they aren't supported by the company culture's practices, norms, values, and assumptions, then these programs will have little impact. Executives can either implement talent initiatives that work within their existing culture or try to change the culture to support the new talent practices and processes they need.

Despite the importance of culture, executives don't always incorporate it into their thinking about talent management. (See the sidebar "How to Make a Culture Diagnosis Useful" on pages 119–20.) You have three options when it comes to culture:

1. Ignore it and hope that cultural norms and practices are aligned enough with management's espoused values to produce the workforce and leadership capabilities you need.
2. Conduct a detailed culture audit to identify where culture change is needed to support the business strategy. Then evaluate talent management options in the context of how they support needed culture change.

3. Take a middle road and make sure your staff understands the top management beliefs and assumptions that
should drive workforce and leadership development.
These cultural principles then become the basis for discussing and evaluating talent initiatives.

Here's how to decide which of these three approaches makes
most sense in your situation.

Ignoring Culture

Some talent programs are so clearly aligned with existing
behaviors in the organization or are so targeted to current
operations that it is safe to simply ignore the implications of
culture. For example, a recruiting program that uses more
aggressive methods to pursue new hires may not have a bear-
ing on other organizational behaviors, practices, or processes.
Consistently ignoring the interactions between culture and
talent management initiatives, however, means culture will
sometimes seriously undermine objectives. For example, a
large defense contractor invested in developing the mentoring
skills of its senior systems engineers because they held knowledge critical to the development of future products. But leaders ignored norms that required engineers to charge their time
to client projects. Since time spent mentoring junior engineers
was rarely viewed as chargeable to a client program, the new
mentoring skills were seldom used. Ignoring cultural practices
or norms that directly conflict with talent management objectives is sure to reduce the payoff from these initiatives.

Using Culture Change to Drive Talent Investments

At the other extreme, leaders often recognize that major culture changes are necessary to drive their business strategy,
and new workforce and leadership capabilities are usually a

How to Make a Culture Diagnosis Useful

"Culture" is a widely used—and often misunderstood—concept. It actually exists on multiple levels:

Practices or *artifacts* are the most visible symbols or manifestations of culture. They describe any widely understood set of repetitive behaviors found in a specific organization. For example, how employees interact in meetings, orient new hires, conduct performance reviews, or respond to customer problems. Culture at this level also includes the tangible systems, processes, procedures, office layout, and so on that influence behaviors and interactions.

Norms are the generally accepted rules of behavior. That is, "the way things are *actually* done around here." Every established organization has unwritten norms about how employees answer e-mail, share information, interact with superiors, treat deadlines, and so on. This is an important element of culture, but it is not enough to focus on just norms and practices.

Values are the essence of culture. They are preferences about what the organization should strive to attain and how it should do so. Values drive behaviors. But it gets complicated because values can be espoused and widely recognized or tacit and unacknowledged. *Espoused* values are things an organization's members will tell you they hold as most important, even though these standards of behavior may clearly conflict with the actual behaviors you observe.[1] Many organizations, for example, claim to value teamwork, employee engagement, and work/life balance. Whether their practices and norms support these values is another thing. Espoused values often conflict with the tacit, widely shared values that actually determine behavior.

(continued)

For example, leaders in a large aerospace company were committed to being a "learning organization," in part, to help retain more young staff members and to accelerate the development of critical systems engineers. To that end, they invested heavily in mentoring programs. But their espoused value of "learning" conflicted directly with the widely accepted and tacit assumption that the best employees were those with the most billable hours. Leadership's refusal to acknowledge and address these conflicting values seriously undermined any investments in mentoring programs.

Executives who want culture to be a boost rather than a barrier in managing talent must make tacit values more explicit, especially when they conflict with your stated objectives for developing workforce and leadership capabilities. Not until tacit beliefs and assumptions are discussable (e.g., "Engineers must be 100 percent billable to client projects") is there any chance of changing organizational priorities or adapting talent initiatives successfully to the existing culture.[2]

major component of these changes. This means talent initiatives are judged in terms of how they support behaviors and capabilities needed in the new culture.

For example, New York Life CEO Ted Mathas faced an increasingly competitive market when he took the top job a few years ago. Data from an employee engagement survey also suggested an increased risk of attrition among newer employees, who chafed at the hierarchical, rules-driven culture. New York Life had grown steadily over the years under a brilliant CEO who created a culture characterized by highly centralized and hierarchical decision making. The new chief executive recognized these cultural norms around decision making and innovation had to evolve if the firm was to aggressively pursue new markets and launch new products faster. Mathas wanted to create a culture that valued distributed decision making, increased innovation, and held managers accountable for talent development.

Thus, talent and leadership initiatives were designed and evaluated based on their ability to support objectives for culture change. A new talent review process was introduced to create a more effective succession pipeline, and the performance management process was redesigned, in part, to begin holding managers accountable for talent development. The new CEO invested considerable time and resources to create a new mind-set among his executive team about what effective leadership meant in the new culture and why it was critical to success. At New York Life, understanding the existing culture's inability to support strategic objectives while identifying new cultural norms and practices needed have defined the talent management and leadership development investments made. In this case, the CEO defined the effectiveness of these initiatives in terms of their ability to support culture change.

No Time or Resources for Culture Change

Most executives don't have the time, resources, or authority to lead a major culture change initiative. But if you still believe that aligning culture is important to talent management success, there is another option.

Let's assume you have already taken an inventory of any existing talent-related programs and processes relevant to your business needs. The next step is to assess your current beliefs and assumptions around talent. These are the principles you hold about what the organization should be doing to build future workforce and leadership capabilities. For example, "We will strive to promote leaders from within." Or, "We don't expect our employees to stay with the company long term." A more detailed list of sample beliefs and assumptions is found in Table 5.2.

Use Table 5.2 to guide a discussion about the cultural and operational norms you expect to drive the talent management efforts in the next one to three years. Follow these steps:

1. Review the entire list one time and delete any of the lines in the table that do not seem relevant. For example, if you don't foresee much hiring, you may delete most or all references to hiring.
2. Add any issues that you expect to encounter but do not see here. For example, if there is a choice between growing in one location or another, you may want to add that choice.
3. Then, for each of the remaining lines in the table, discuss these points:
   - What are some examples of how each side (left or right column) on the continuum might look for your organization?
   - Imagine a "slider" between the left and right columns that is currently in the middle of the continuum. How far would you move this slider toward one side or the other to show your intentions?
   - How would emphasizing one side or the other affect the talent management efforts required to execute on that?

Some of these principles may already be embedded as norms in your organization's culture. That is, they are "the

TABLE 5.2   Cultural Principles Affecting Talent Management

1. Recruit recent college grads	Recruit seasoned professionals
2. Hire from current talent pool	Partner with schools to improve local talent
3. Staff and run own operations	Outsource (non)essential functions wherever possible
4. Hire only full-time employees	Use contractors or temporary help whenever possible
5. Focus on role stability and reducing attrition	Encourage rotational assignments and career mobility across organization
6. Grow leaders from within	Hire experienced executives from competitors and outside industry
7. Promote centralized, consistent leadership and management practices	Develop autonomous work unit approaches to leadership and management
8. Expect self-directed learning and career development	Require standard training and career development programs
9. Require employees to have deep, specialized expertise (specialists)	Encourage employees to have broad knowledge of a variety of areas (generalists)
10. Hire for the long term	Don't expect employees to stay long term
11. Lay off surplus talent quickly	Repurpose headcount from one unit to another to minimize layoffs

(continued)

TABLE 5.2   Cultural Principles Affecting Talent Management (*continued*)

---

12. Reduce population of older, potentially more expensive workers	Actively retain older high performers
13. Pay for seniority	Pay for performance
14. Grow by hiring individuals	Grow through acquisitions and integration of acquired staff
15. Focus talent programs on top managers and future high-potential leaders	Provide broad access to talent programs, to include technical and critical roles
16. Support affinity groups	Limited support for affinity groups
17. Buy industry best talent programs	Build low-cost, homegrown talent programs
18. Foster collaboration at local level	Foster national or international collaboration
19. Make talent decisions based on extensive data	Analyze limited data
20. Staff centralized work sites	Staff decentralized or virtual work sites
21. Top down, traditional communication of business strategy	Enterprisewide direct-to-employee communication of strategy
Add your own cultural principle	

way we do things around here." For example, maybe you already tend to promote leaders from within the organization and you expect to continue doing so. Other principles related to talent management may be new to the organization, such as "We retain high-performing older workers as long as possible." Perhaps historically, your firm encouraged older workers to retire as soon as they were eligible, but now skill shortages make that a less productive norm. As a leader, you want to make this new principle known to your managers and talent management team, or at least debate it explicitly, so everybody reaches agreement on what the key operating principles should be.

When a small high-tech firm encouraged its leaders to discuss the beliefs and assumptions shown in Table 5.2, three lessons were clear:

1. Choices driving talent strategies are likely to vary by unit or even specific roles. For example, in this company, consulting services had to recruit seasoned professionals with specialized knowledge from a broad geographic area, while the centralized operations of technical support required hiring younger staff locally who could be trained on the firm's proprietary technology. This meant the two functions needed different types of recruiting support to build and sustain future capabilities. Top management realized that a one-size-fits-all system was counterproductive.

2. Some existing cultural practices clearly were not working. Leaders had assumed, for example, that training in the company should be self-directed, which was the current norm. But evidence showed this approach was not effective. Executives realized that more structured,

required training had to become standard practice in the culture. They realized that the existing norm around self-directed training was keeping the firm from bidding on hundreds of thousands of dollars in contracts annually because they lacked a quick and nimble way of adding resources to scale up their capacity.

3. Executives also gained insights into workforce and leadership issues they needed to monitor in the future. For example, discussions with the head of HR about growing versus recruiting leaders yielded agreement about the need to create a process to identify and develop high potentials for future leadership roles. There was also agreement on the need to invest in new programs to retain older workers nearing retirement, at least on a part-time basis. Progress on talent management initiatives related to these issues could now be tracked as a regular agenda item in meetings with HR.

Discussions intended to make talent-related beliefs and assumptions explicit don't take a great deal of time. They will only draw on a subset of the choices in Table 5.2. Executives using the list should focus on the dimensions most relevant to their situations. Some decisions are inevitably made at a corporate level and may be out of your control. Others must be made at the business unit or departmental level. Of course, you can add your own items to the list.

Use the relevant assumptions and beliefs in Table 5.2 to improve the cultural fit of existing and potential talent initiatives in your organization. Treat each item as a dimension and communicate what you want more or less of. Specific benefits of generating a dialog around these principles include the following:

- By making your assumptions and beliefs explicit, you increase the chances your managers and HR staff will address talent problems in ways most effective for the organization and important subunits. There will often be no clear black-or-white answers to the questions posed, but you can identify where the organization fits on a continuum or where it needs to be. (For example, we expect to promote 70 to 80 percent of leaders from within versus we are likely to promote 20 to 30 percent from within.)
- You can identify which existing norms and practices are undermining talent-related objectives. Only then can you target specific aspects of culture for change or adapt initiatives to work better in the existing environment.
- You can use this discussion about culturally related assumptions and beliefs to identify new problem areas that need attention to formulate a more comprehensive talent management agenda going forward.

Clarifying the current state of your talent management investments and assessing their cultural fit are not glamorous executive tasks, but they will provide significant payoffs for the business. Stopping costly, unproductive programs, realigning others to make sure they support business objectives, and identifying major gaps in existing efforts are all actions that can add tremendous value. And they set you up for the next step in the process, which is exploring and evaluating innovative solutions that will be essential for long-term success. Exploring these state-of-the-art solutions is the focus of Chapters 6 and 7.

For Talent Management and HR Business Partners

Understand What You Have and Who You Are

For the HR manager, this chapter is all about understanding and working with current reality. The reality of talent management as it is happening now and the reality of your corporate culture as it is—or as leaders want it to be.

That's where an inventory of talent management activities comes in. In this chapter, we have advised executives to ask you for an inventory, but you don't have to wait for top managers or executives to ask you. Always be ready to present a full accounting of all your talent management activities and how they relate to business strategy. As a talent management leader, you need a full grasp of what is happening under your direction, as well as what you're doing personally. You must understand your customers (that is, your business unit executives), know how your success is being measured, and be able to defend the services you are offering or supporting in terms of their contribution to the business.

Remember the inventory is simply a list of all the activities that support having a ready workforce and leadership team. This includes the work done formally by your group, as well as the informal or ad hoc activities done by others in the organization.

Once you have this list, ask yourself these questions:

- Which programs are most important to delivering on our business strategy?
- Which are redundant?
- Which need additional resources?
- Which need stronger political support or sponsorship?

- Which should be cancelled or cut?
- Which could be consolidated to increase quality and efficiency?
- Which need to be carefully monitored? Which require little supervision?
- Which ones are so strong that they should be presented at an executive staff meeting or shared with colleagues in other divisions?

When you can answer these questions, you show that you are a good steward of all talent management resources whether or not they are under your direct control. You gain credibility by thinking and acting as an executive in charge of talent management.

You can also take your stewardship beyond programs that are under your direct control. Even for talent management activities that don't report to you, such as training budgets under the control of individual managers, you should be able to find ways to add value. Simply by consolidating information about talent management activities, you demonstrate a broader awareness of the business and the ability to work through others to improve talent management. By improving information sharing in this way, you will find yourself increasingly called upon to consult with line managers on talent issues.

Culture

In looking at culture, your position is different. You are not the executive who is driving the culture; you are the innovator who needs to understand the culture, or the goals for the culture,

(continued)

in order to effectively ensure appropriate talent management activities.

Since culture is often more a "feeling" than any stated truths, your job is to help executives articulate what culture means—to turn your typical practices, norms, values, tacit assumptions, and so on into actionable decision rules. Using Table 5.2, start by eliminating the choices that are less relevant to your business. You might settle on just a handful as most important. Then, think about factors related to your market, region, products, or employees. What other cultural choices are important and unique to your situation that you should add to the list we've provided?

Answer these questions and then try to imagine how your top executives would describe your culture relative to the choices on each line. With that background, have a conversation with your leaders to see how closely your interpretations match. In some cases you'll find that where you currently land on the continuum of each line is not where the organization needs to be. You'll be able to use this discussion to further prioritize and focus your subsequent plans for talent management—supporting the best elements of the current culture and making changes to improve the culture as appropriate.

6

Innovative Solutions

Recruiting, Retention, and
the Role of Technology

A financial services firm needed its talent management infrastructure to more efficiently support the hiring and development of several thousand new employees each year. This process included evaluating the pool of more than 50,000 résumés the company received annually. The executive responsible for fixing the problem had heard good things about the capabilities of several technology vendors selling "talent management solutions," and his staff was currently evaluating proposals for these new IT applications. But this senior manager had no experience judging these types of investments in talent management infrastructure, and he wanted to make sure his HR department made the right decision.

In other organizations, top management must sometimes pay special attention to retaining highly skilled professionals already on staff. Leaders of a large medical center and teaching hospital in rural North Carolina, for example, had a business strategy that called for continued growth. But to expand its delivery of cutting-edge medical practices, management knew that, with an aging workforce and the difficulties of recruiting young staff in a rural environment, the hospital had to retain its experienced nurses. Keeping these veterans engaged was the key to training new nurses and to sustaining high-quality patient care. Focus groups with the older nurses revealed many felt "burned out" and even resentful of the sign-on bonuses and extra attention going to new hires. To achieve their growth objectives, leaders had to find ways to increase the engagement and retention of this veteran group.

When it comes to managing talent and developing leaders, the array of problems and potential innovative solutions can be daunting. For executives the question is, How can you ensure that your subordinates make effective new investments to meet these challenges? The next two chapters describe some of the most creative approaches we've found at different stages of the talent management life cycle. They won't make you an expert in all areas of talent management, but these solutions will give you a sense of options to explore. This chapter concentrates on solutions for getting and retaining high-performing employees, and the role information technology can play in maximizing your talent investments. Chapter 7 focuses on innovative solutions for transferring knowledge and accelerating development of employees at all levels to help meet performance and retention objectives. As you go through the examples in these two chapters, look at the way the problems and solutions are framed and at the vocabulary used. This will help you frame your own challenges and analyze the solutions presented to you.

Microsoft's Intern Program Improves Its "Quality of Hire"

To stay competitive with the likes of Google, Cisco, and HP, Microsoft must continually attract and retain supersmart talent fresh out of the world's leading universities. But the competition for this small, elite talent pool of graduates in disciplines such as computer science, engineering, and marketing has continued to heat up. So Microsoft has increasingly relied on its college intern program as a major source of qualified candidates. The company hires more than 1,000 interns annually, most of whom work on the main campus in Redmond, Washington. Microsoft recognizes that interns are creative, energetic, and hard workers, but they are not cheap labor. Interns are paid competitive wages, and the company also covers expenses for relocation, training, and social events. The intern program's primary objectives are to:

- Identify, qualify, and attract potential full-time hires
- Prepare and orient potential new hires to be highly productive when they join the company
- Create "believers" out of talented students who return to campus after their internships and sell Microsoft to their peers
- Build strong relationships at top schools with faculty and staff who continue to encourage their students to consider Microsoft internships and jobs

Microsoft knows that the best intern experiences start with a committed executive who holds hiring managers accountable for meeting the firm's commitments to its interns. Microsoft's primary promise to the program's participants is that they will be assigned meaningful work. This means assigning them to projects comparable to what might be done by a new full-time employee. The projects must also develop the intern's skills, so he or she is learning throughout the program. This learning comes, in part, from weekly performance feedback that their manager must provide, so interns have an opportunity to show improvement. In one sense, the intern program is a prolonged job interview where participants are evaluated on their ability to adapt to new challenges, interact with a team, solve problems, and produce results.

But Microsoft also makes a strong effort to help interns integrate comfortably into the firm's culture. An onboarding program helps participants decode the company's culture and gives them the practical tools they need to succeed in what, for many, is their first office job. At the same time, the company hosts barbeques and other social events throughout the summer that allow interns to build relationships with their peers, future coworkers, and senior leaders from across the company. Top managers also make an effort to meet each intern personally during these social events and informal executive lunches.

Ultimately, Microsoft's goal is to give its interns an experience that translates into a great story they will tell again and again when they return to school. Executives track the success of the program through a series of metrics. These include:

- Percentage of interns who eventually accept full-time employment with Microsoft
- A method for tracking how former interns perform as full-time employees over time, compared to peers who were not interns and experienced hires who join from

other software companies (Former interns routinely out-perform peers in the other groups.)

- Exit surveys that show interns' perceptions of Microsoft after they return to school
- Percentage of recruited students from target schools that accept full-time employment offers from Microsoft instead of going to a competitor

Intern programs have become increasingly popular among organizations that need to recruit scarce talent. To separate your program from competitors, make sure your staff is paying close attention to the details that create the interns' experience—and the story they will tell. Ultimately, that's what determines the measure that matters most—committed, high-quality new hires who can be productive immediately.

Onboarding at Electronic Arts

Bringing new hires into the organization, and getting them oriented and productive as fast as possible, is one step in the overall talent management process where many organizations have consistently missed opportunities. Overly bureaucratic, information-intensive programs designed by HR departments often leave new employees overloaded with marginally rel-evant information and unable to readily access the things they need to become productive quickly. Leaders who have any questions about the effectiveness of their current onboarding process should assess employees who have joined the company in the last 6 to 18 months. Find out if these new employees are capable of doing the tasks they were hired to do, if they can answer the "big picture" questions about your strategy (as outlined in Chapter 3), how engaged or satisfied they are, and whether or not they intend to stay.

Like many fast-growing high-tech firms, Electronic Arts, one of the world's leading interactive game companies, faced a serious challenge in onboarding hundreds of new employees annually. To get new hires productive in development studios and offices at more than 15 sites around the world took from 5 to 30 days and included a series of classroom orientations, along with a listing of Web resources. But new employees were often overwhelmed with the volume of information delivered, which did little to make them productive faster and also created a frustrating initiation to the company. In this highly competitive market that demands rapid new product development, EA's leaders needed to improve the firm's onboarding process to accelerate productivity.

Part of the solution for the firm's onboarding challenge has come from its major investment in two technology platforms. EA Knowledge, the company's online knowledge base, is an electronic library of articles, blogs, videos, and other information, used by many new hires to find information they need to be productive. This knowledge base is integrated with a social networking portal, known as EA People, that helps the company's 9,000 employees collaborate more effectively across the global company and accelerate the rapid development of more innovative new games.

Both EA People and EA Knowledge have user communities where new employees can quickly find the personal connections and information they need to be productive. New software engineers and artists, for example, can join an "animation" group where they can download videos they need to watch, find training on key software programs, and refer to best practices they need to know. They can also find links to other groups, useful websites, and ways to connect with others at EA doing similar work. The firm's leaders are very aware that their young staff learns differently than older generations, so it tries to apply technologies to take advantage of these new learning styles. "Converting onboarding into an e-learning environment enables new employees to digest a vast amount of information when they are ready to assimilate it," said one EA executive.[1]

Even when the onboarding activity is highly structured, like the programs at EA, the questions are the same: Are new employees capable of doing the tasks they were hired to do? Can they answer the big picture questions about your company strategy? How satisfied are they? Do they intend to stay? Don't get distracted by the details of the talent management program, however forward-looking or sophisticated. Keep focused on your goal of a prepared, strategically savvy, and engaged workforce.

Westpac Bank Drives Talent Management with Technology Investments

As evidenced at EA, information technology is central to many talent management processes and practices, just as it has become the backbone of many HR capabilities. But how the technology is selected, implemented, and applied varies tremendously from organization to organization. IT applications in talent management are heavily influenced by:

- **Legacy technology infrastructure.** Does every talent application have to integrate with your SAP or HRIS system? Do you have multiple HR systems resulting from acquisitions? Does this IT application have to integrate with existing talent systems?
- **Number and complexity of roles being filled.** Are you running a high-skill, distributed global R&D operation or staffing call centers or retail stores with high turnover?
- **Organization's culture.** Are you in a high-tech firm where many tasks are already done online? Or is yours a reasonably low-tech business where supervisors insist they are too busy to go online?
- **Competition and cost of recruiting and retaining talent.** Is your highly skilled talent very expensive to recruit and hard to retain? Or is talent readily available and turnover expected?

In reality, most executives will play a very limited role in the design, selection, and implementation of IT systems that drive talent management processes and practices. But that doesn't mean leaders should simply abdicate these decisions to HR and IT functions. If you are in a position to influence these investments, there are some assumptions you should challenge and questions to ask that can add considerable value to decisions about technology investments. First, here's an example of an organization that has implemented IT-based talent management solutions.

Westpac Banking Corporation is one of Australia's largest employers and is constantly ranked as one of the world's best financial services companies. But to sustain this competitive position, Westpac's leaders have had to pay special attention to its ability to attract and retain the highly skilled workers needed to deliver its customer-focused strategy. That's because the pool of available talent has shrunk dramatically with only 175,000 workers expected to enter the Australian workforce between 2010 and 2020. (That number used to be 175,000 *per year.*) In addition, exit interviews showed that almost 20 percent of Westpac's employees who voluntarily left the bank quit because of a lack of perceived career opportunities. Finally, supervisors and managers made it clear that the existing process for hiring internal job candidates was so arduous that they preferred to hire external candidates. Thus, the tightening labor market made talent retention a critical strategic issue for Westpac's leaders.[2]

As part of the solution for addressing these problems, the bank's "Workforce of the Future" initiative included the implementation of Careers@Westpac, a set of new recruiting and career management processes that used software applications from Taleo, a leading supplier of talent management technology systems. In Australia, Westpac used the capabilities in Taleo's software to consolidate all internal job postings electronically and to redesign its internal hiring process. Westpac had a different need in its New Zealand operations, however, where the emphasis was on external hiring. The new technology provided capabilities such as:

- Employees could create and maintain their own skill-based profiles electronically. Information on potential candidates was tracked in a structured database.
- When positions become available, the system creates a short list of qualified candidates for hiring managers.

- Potential candidates are automatically notified of openings by e-mail.
- Alerts are sent to candidates throughout the process updating them on their application status.
- Many reports, including "new hire" and "requisition status" reports, are easily produced to provide management visibility across the enterprise.

The automation of recruiting and career management processes at Westpac was actually part of a larger culture change initiative led by CEO David Morgan. Westpac's leaders wanted to develop a culture that supported more effective use of the bank's existing talent. This meant increasing the mobility and visibility of high-performing employees across the company, while also creating an expectation that individuals would take responsibility for their own career development, using resources provided by the bank.

The CEO played a major role in communicating these new expectations throughout the bank. The communications strategy included an emphasis on the new career management capabilities available to both hiring managers and employees provided by the Taleo applications. Management also conducted a series of focus groups with employees to find out how they were experiencing the capabilities provided. Use of the new system was reinforced with an ongoing traveling program for employees based on the theme "What do I want to be when I grow up?" These events focused on how employees could use the career management application in the Careers@ Westpac initiative. Finally, a team of internal HR consultants provided ongoing support to Westpac's hiring managers in using the system to improve the internal hiring and redeployment process.

The benefits of the new Careers@Westpac service were almost immediately evident. The system played a central role in supporting the bank's culture change initiative. Concepts of internal mobility and the redeployment of talent when teams restructured became the new standard for how the organization functioned. Significant cost savings resulted because of the increased tendency to hire internally. These savings were possible because of the new processes now available to redeploy staff more efficiently, which also reduced costly layoffs.

The new recruiting and career development systems at Westpac are examples of the value technology can add in improving talent management capabilities. But there are many variations on how the technology can be applied to support talent-related objectives. Top management can play an important role making sure these IT investments are successful by challenging assumptions and asking key questions of the project team. Five areas where questions should almost always be asked are:

1. **How will the outputs or benefits of this technology-based "talent management solution" clearly support our business objectives? Will this system help us run the business better or identify and address talent-related threats to performance? Or is this system primarily for compliance purposes?** A surprising number of these investments focus more tactically on cutting costs in recruiting or training processes (e.g., reducing "time-to-hire") and on compliance issues, instead of focusing on

improving business performance, which can be reflected in a measure like "quality of hire."

2. **What are we doing about the behavioral or cultural changes that will be required if managers and employees are to use these applications effectively? Are these changes being done *to* employees or *with* employees?** Many large companies have installed talent management applications that their employees won't use because they are too cumbersome and time consuming. Westpac's leaders, for example, recognized that implementation of new recruiting and career management processes required significant behavioral changes, which is why the system was part of a large culture change initiative led by the CEO.

3. **How does this technology investment fit into our overall talent management strategy? Is this system going to promote long-term integration—or unification—of talent processes? Or is it worth supporting as a standalone system because the benefits are so great?** Many HR departments are still balkanized (e.g., compensation doesn't talk to recruiting), and they fall into the trap of pursuing isolated technology solutions, which are counterproductive in the long term.

4. **How will this system integrate with our legacy human resource information systems, enterprise systems, or existing talent applications? Is the CIO on board with this investment?** These can be politically charged questions in some organizations where talent program sponsors may be trying an end run around legacy IT investments that now feel like a huge barrier to innovation.

5. **How many executive sponsors have we talked to at existing customers for the vendors we are considering? How do their objectives and organizational context compare to ours?** Vendors selling talent management software are popping up left and right because of the exploding demand in this field. Of course, vendors will have different strengths in different application areas. Make sure the one your team chooses has a proven track record. And, if you are outsourcing particular capabilities to a vendor or are going the "software as a service" (SaaS) route, make sure your new supplier has its own talent management plan. How will your vendor sustain its own critical capabilities long term? Ask your team what its "off ramp" plan is if the vendor can't deliver these outsourced capabilities over time.

Information technology will play an increasingly central role in managing talent in the years ahead. But, like other promising IT opportunities, this field will be littered with wasted investments. You can greatly decrease your chances of making these costly mistakes if you:

- Require clear and sustained links to business objectives
- Pay serious attention to the behavioral changes needed to make the system successful
- Refuse to ignore challenges of integration with overall talent and technology systems

The best way to succeed with these technology investments is to ask the hard questions up front and hold out for acceptable answers.

Reengaging Older Workers to Improve Performance

Leaders in a growing number of industries must confront the fact that there are not enough younger skilled professionals or experienced managers to fill the roles being vacated by retiring baby boomers. However, this is a very patchwork problem. In some areas, top management can't wait for veteran staff to retire and to replace them with younger employees. But, in the last generation, both the private and public sectors have created a great number of professional and managerial roles that will be extremely hard to fill in the years ahead. For example, systems engineers, geoscientists, risk managers, network architects, tool and die makers, and nurse managers are just some of the key roles management will struggle to fill with experienced, highly skilled replacements when these predecessors leave. In some cases, inability to fill these jobs will have a direct impact on strategic performance, as discussed in Chapter 4. Here's a creative example showing how leaders in one organization have invested in a program that helps retain older professionals in key roles.

Top management at Pitt County Memorial Hospital (PCMH) in North Carolina realized that the hospital's plans for continued growth depended in part on its ability to retain its veteran nurses. Recruiting nurses to poor rural regions like eastern North Carolina has proved very challenging, which makes retaining experienced nurses even more critical. Thus, PCMH created an annual program to help 25 of its most highly regarded veteran nurses rethink their practices and their careers within the health system. The three-day off-site is designed to keep nurses at the bedside, but also to acquaint participants with opportunities to grow in areas of leadership, research, professional development, and community service.

Of course, the program, known as "Fanning the Flame," has been part of a larger set of initiatives that PCMH pursued to implement an overall performance improvement strategy. Of 144 graduates in the first six years of the program, only 4 left the health system.[3]

The first day of the program, which is held at a quiet seaside retreat, is devoted to helping participants de-stress. Relaxation techniques that include massage, beachcombing, humor, and quiet time are used to disconnect from hectic work and family lives. The second day reinforces the value these professionals bring to the hospital as part of an effective team. Participants also hear from other nurses like themselves who have pursued growth opportunities such as conducting research, taking on new leadership roles, participating in clinical teaching programs, or pursuing advanced nursing degrees. The last day of the program focuses on "job sculpting," where participants create new goals for themselves and leave with a plan for how they will rethink their practices and careers.

Fanning the Flame helps reengage and retain veteran professionals by:

1. Fueling their imagination about alternative opportunities for growth within the organization
2. Showing that the organization is trying to help them succeed as individuals
3. Sustaining the motivation for growth through annual reunions of all the program's graduates
4. Helping nurses develop new, meaningful personal relationships with high-performing colleagues from other parts of the hospital system

Fanning the Flame costs about $1,800 per participant. This is a good investment, since the cost of replacing one veteran nurse is about $65,000, not to mention the hidden costs of having unmotivated veterans at work. Among participants, 73 percent reported the program influenced their decisions to continue working within the hospital system. "I was just doing my time and getting closer to retirement," said one veteran nurse. "But this program gave me incentives to improve myself. It was the difference between keeping a stagnant employee versus one who is now continuing to improve."

When you look at an innovative program like this one, continue to ask the most basic business case questions to evaluate efficacy.

Using Retirees to Improve Productivity and Innovation

One study found that 62 percent of organizations surveyed were currently hiring retired employees as consultants or temporary workers.[4] This trend will certainly continue and even accelerate as the overall talent pool shrinks in the years ahead.

Some organizations will make a strategic decision to actively pursue retirees—either their own or from other companies—to fill relatively low-skilled positions. In fact, companies such as Staples, Safeway, and Citizens Bank are already using this staffing strategy because they believe older workers interact well with older customers and turn over at a substantially lower rate, says Tim Driver, CEO of RetirementJobs. com. But an even greater opportunity may be finding ways to reconnect with retirees who have specialized expertise or leadership capabilities to fill critical short-term needs. The majority of organizations today that rehire employees who are collecting retirement benefits do so on a case-by-case basis. Employees return as part-time contractors or consultants based on their personal relationship with a particular manager or executive.

Some organizations, like the Aerospace Corporation in El Segundo, California, have formalized the process of utilizing the expertise of their retirees in providing technical analysis and assessments for national security and commercial space programs. (Aerospace created a formal program when it noticed that too many employees were retiring and then coming back as consultants at rates higher than their salaries at retirement—management needed to get its consulting costs under control.) Today, the firm's Retiree Casual program has about 300 retirees providing expertise that supports projects to test, analyze, and troubleshoot virtually every aspect of rocket and satellite systems. This program has become a critical resource to meet the firm's changing needs for highly trained and experienced engineers.[5]

Rehiring recent retirees, or hiring retirees from other organizations, addresses five immediate issues:

- Is the easiest and cheapest way to fill a critical skills or capability gap
- Avoids time and resources needed to train a replacement
- May provide the only source of unique knowledge needed to sustain performance
- May buy more time to transfer knowledge to successors
- Can be a source of special value-added knowledge needed to spark new product or process innovation

Though the benefits of bringing in veteran expertise are clear, there are also some risks. Many companies have been hesitant to hire retirees because of uncertainty about laws and pension regulations that seem to discourage employing retirees.

Such concerns are addressed by YourEncore.com, a firm originally spun off by Procter & Gamble and Eli Lilly to build and manage a portfolio of retired engineers and scientists. In recent years, some 5,000 experts have become available to YourEncore's network of more than 50 member companies. Firms like Boeing, Kraft, General Mills, and Johnson & Johnson now tap into this specialized knowledge resource on a project basis. YourEncore, which serves as the employer of record for the retired experts, provides several valuable services for firms who join its network. First, they establish and maintain programs to help companies catalogue and access their own retirees to retain critical knowledge. Eli Lilly uses Your Encore to access retired engineers and scientists for up to 100 projects a year in its R&D function. They have also proved to be a resource for accelerating innovation by providing firms with access to unique expertise from outside their industry.

For example, P&G hired a former Boeing systems engineer who brought his knowledge of virtual modeling to the problem of designing and testing a new diaper product. Applying this expertise to the product development process enabled P&G to launch its new product almost a year ahead of schedule, capturing major market share and millions of dollars in new revenue.

Given the looming shortages in technical and scientific expertise, as more baby boomers retire, leaders will find themselves increasingly challenged to find new experienced resources to meet strategic objectives, while also containing costs. Thus, the notion of fully utilizing retirees will become increasingly appealing where it makes economic sense. When approached about initiatives in this area, here are some questions to keep in mind:

- By hiring retirees, are we getting capabilities that we need to sustain long term, or only temporarily?
- If these retirees are providing capabilities needed in the long term, how will this initiative ensure their skills and knowledge are transferred to younger employees?
- Is this initiative creating a standard process for bringing retirees back to work here?
- How do the costs and benefits of this solution compare to other alternatives considered?

This chapter has focused on innovative solutions at the beginning and the end of the talent life cycle. We have also tried to show how to think effectively about the role IT should play throughout the process. Recruiting and onboarding young talent and maximizing the productivity of veteran workers are all going to be key leverage points in this era of a changing workforce. But even more important is going to be bridging the capability gap between experienced employees and their successors. That's why Chapter 7 focuses on creative approaches to accelerate the development of the critical professionals and leaders who will be the key to your organization's future.

For Talent Management and HR Business Partners

Keeping Up with Innovations in Talent Management

Every day, creative leaders are coming up with new ideas for effectively recruiting, onboarding, developing, and retaining employees. How do you know you're keeping up? To gauge your knowledge of the latest developments, answer the following questions:

- Can you speak the language of talent management? Whether you agree with them or not, what is your understanding of the 10 most popular and current buzzwords in your industry? Are you able to define those same buzzwords in layperson's terms as well?
- Can you identify three to five companies in your country or region that are similar to your organization and then describe what they are doing in talent management? For example, have you reached out to a company in a different industry that is similar to yours and learned what it does for talent management?
- Can you describe some new ideas your company is *not* adopting—and explain why in the context of your big picture strategy these approaches don't make sense for you?
- Are you familiar with the current thinking on *long-standing* concepts in talent management, such as onboarding, improving employee engagement, and so on? Once you implement an idea, do you keep up with how other organizations are using that tool or concept today?
- What is your approach to technology? Do you tend to look to technology as a first solution to every HR problem?

Or do you avoid solutions that involve new technologies? Can you say how that bias affects the talent management activities that you tend to pursue?

- When you look at new solutions, do you tie back your analysis to your big picture strategy and risk analysis? Can you show that the solutions you're presenting are connected to strategy and risk?

- How do you decide that a new technique is more effective than something that has been used in the past?

Keep in mind that *new* does not always mean "more effective." When looking at talent management choices, you should look at new ideas as rigorously as you would more traditional methods. Just because a solution employs social networking or is mobile-enabled, for example, does not mean that it is the correct choice. Remember that a few years ago everyone was excited about knowledge management systems and competency models. Recently, the cachet of those concepts has waned.

For ideas on sharing innovative solutions with executives, see Chapter 7's comment, "For Talent Management and HR Business Partners: Presenting Talent Management Innovations to Executives."

7

Innovative Solutions

Accelerating Knowledge Transfer and Leadership Development

A senior financial executive for a major manufacturing company was retiring at a critical time for the firm. The organization had been doing a lot of short-term financing to maintain its cash flow, and this highly respected leader had incredibly strong connections throughout the banking world. The firm's CEO knew it was imperative that the successor to this retiring executive move into his new role seamlessly to maintain strong relationships with major lenders. Anything less would threaten the firm's critical short-term financing arrangements and its cash flow. About 40 percent of executives hired fail within the first 18 months, and about 25 percent of internal hires don't make it.[1] Each failed top-level transition can cost an organization millions of dollars, not counting lost productivity. The CEO of this manufacturing firm wanted to ensure the transition of his new finance executive would be successful.

In another case, a multinational apparel company wanted to focus its most creative project managers on more strategic and challenging projects. Executives decided to outsource the management of more predictable projects to an existing group of vendor partners in Asia. If this worked well, the company planned to roll out the outsourced project manager structures throughout Asia. Hundreds of millions of dollars were on the line because the project managers' performance affects product quality, supply chain efficiency, time to market, and consumer acceptance. Even for the most standard apparel, project managers have to be able to understand the nuances of a variety of situations, be it a supply chain problem or a design conflict. They also have to juggle the conflicting requirements of key players, including designers, marketing staff, and product developers. To make its new structure work, the apparel company needed to find a way to help its outsourced project managers absorb the cultural sensitivity, tacit knowledge, and troubleshooting mind-set of the in-house product managers. The senior leader for all of Taiwan and Korea needed an effective way to transfer this complex knowledge so outsource partners could bring those in the new project management roles up to speed quickly.

Given the dramatic changes coming in the talent pool, a lot of organizations today are investing in pretty mundane, "me-too" talent development initiatives. Do you have standard onboarding programs for key new hires; a little bit of e-learning to jazz up leadership development; an online, automated career management module; and a half-baked mentoring program? That's not enough!

If you look honestly at your existing talent pipeline and the increasing competition to accelerate the development of highly skilled professionals and promising young leaders, you're going to have to invest a lot more in innovative solutions, as compared to the standard ones, to get the capabilities you'll need in the future. To accomplish this task, you need to know about the more creative approaches available to clarify roles and accelerate learning that addresses the talent risks your organization is facing. That's what this chapter delivers. We'll show you powerful examples of how:

- Pfizer used a custom transition process to improve the success rate of key new executives
- A major clothing retailer clarified recruiting and development needs for critical new roles needed to support growth
- A U.S. government R&D lab taught its scientists to be truly effective mentors
- Companies like Google, P&G, and The Franciscan Health System successfully accelerate leadership development

Pfizer: Improving Success Rate of Executive Transitions

Some talent management-related initiatives, like the IT investments described in Chapter 6, affect large segments of the workforce. In other cases, a solution is needed that focuses on a strategically important group, or even a specific individual. A small group of consultants, for example, now specializes in reducing the risks of key leadership transitions. Research has consistently shown that more than one-third of senior executives new to their roles fail within 18 months.[2] The costs of these failed transitions can be tremendous, so smart leaders are increasingly willing to invest more resources to ensure that senior managers will be effective in their new roles.

"If you just see these changes as onboarding a new leader, that's a wasted opportunity," said Carlota Vollhardt, president of Executive Knowledge International, a firm that specializes in facilitating top management transitions. "These transitions are a prime opportunity to help the business move in a new strategic direction." This process makes sure the incoming executive is quickly educated about where the real minefields—and opportunities—are located when entering into a new role.

For example, Pfizer used this customized succession process to fill a senior position in one of its major pharmaceutical businesses when a key executive was promoted to the head of a function.[3] The successor, who was moving from another division, would be advising the president of one of the company's major businesses on complex legal and regulatory issues. Interviews with key stakeholders, who had worked with her predecessor and who knew the role she was taking over, identified key success factors for the new executive. For example, certain gaps in the successor's industry knowledge were uncovered that needed to be addressed immediately. In addition, interviews with colleagues of the executive leaving the position revealed that his use of a largely invisible external network of key advisors had been critical to his success. This network would have gone unnoticed in a normal transition. Once identified, however, the departing executive was asked to personally introduce his successor to some of these key advisors so she could begin building her own relationships within this network of experts.

Two key metrics chosen for monitoring the overall effectiveness of this transition were (1) attrition on the new executive's team and (2) level of client satisfaction, which in this case was that of the division president. There was no attrition on the team, and the division president reported being very pleased with the service and expertise received from the new leader and her team. This is an example of a custom intervention that can have considerable payoffs in high-risk executive transitions.

When your situation is amorphous, as it was for Pfizer, return to the fundamental business case questions to evaluate the special-purpose talent management plan: Who is the "customer" for the solution? Whom does it serve? What does it cost? Can you articulate a clear link to business objectives? How long will it take? How will you measure success? What is the plan for long-term maintenance?

R&D Lab: Creating Mentors Who Can Actually Teach

Senior executive transitions are only one of many situations in talent management that requires effective knowledge transfer. It's no secret that the most effective way to transfer complex, experiential (or tacit) knowledge is through personal mentoring between veteran and less experienced employees. Of course, with a more global workforce, these interactions may be increasingly mediated through technology via audio- and videoconferences, e-mail and text messaging, and so on. No matter what communication medium is used, one problem remains when it comes to knowledge transfer between individuals: those with the specific knowledge often don't know how to teach it to others. When mentors can't teach effectively, many of their interactions with a less experienced employee are a waste of time.

Thus, organizations can significantly improve many talent-related activities by improving the ability of their experienced employees and managers to mentor or teach. "Mentor," in this context, means short-term skill building and knowledge transfer. It means those who know how to do a job teaching those who need to know, so they can be productive faster. Unfortunately, the concept of "mentoring" has gained a bad reputation among many executives who have been victimized by well-intentioned but unfocused and unproductive initiatives that have produced little or no business impact.

Our own training and consulting experience, however, has shown that mentoring programs can be highly effective, both in terms of accelerated individual development and improved business performance. For example, we worked with one U.S. government R&D lab that knew certain strategic capabilities were at risk if management didn't find ways to help veteran engineers and scientists share their unique technical knowledge before retiring. The lab also had young staff members who needed extensive training in esoteric aspects of its work before they could become productive. To retain critical knowledge and accelerate development of the young staff, 60 lab employees participated in a workshop called "Peer Mentoring: A Practical Approach to Knowledge Transfer."[4] In the full day session, participants learned how to:

- Define their roles and responsibilities as mentors, apprentices, or managers
- Clarify the best ways to communicate with each other during the busy workday

- Break their jobs down into manageable chunks to iden-tify what to teach
- Create a measurable plan for transferring skills
- Teach job content more effectively by considering appren-tices' learning styles
- Ask test questions to ensure the content was actually learned
- Provide feedback on the resulting work

One of the immediate benefits of this skill-building work-shop was that a senior chemist began working with three junior staff members, teaching them the basis of toxic sub-stance testing. As a result, the young team was able to bring an unused testing lab back online to pursue several strategic projects. The team also began using the lab to save on costly external testing. The leader who sponsored the mentoring ini-tiative concluded:

> *When you implement a mentoring program, you need to look at your strategic objectives because you've got to decide where to concentrate. We have a lot of new employees com-ing on board, and our senior people have limited time to teach them. But with this mentoring program, a protocol is being established for what has to be done to get a new person up to speed faster so they're productive.*

When asked to consider an investment in a mentoring pro-gram, you want to know what the apprentice will be able to *do* at the end of the mentoring relationship. The mentor/apprentice relationship should always be defined in terms of a problem or question the pair can work on. When a men-tor and apprentice come together to solve a problem, such as how to present a creative idea or how to negotiate a C-level contract, the mentor more easily sees how he or she can help. This contrasts with mentoring that is focused on relationship building only, where there is no foundation of shared work. If a proposed investment in mentoring doesn't define the learning that should take place, then you are likely to have veteran employees shying away from signing up or to find yourself dissatisfied with the results.

Major Retailer: Defining a Critical Role to Accelerate Recruiting and Development

Organizations today have many roles where complex skill sets and tacit knowledge make it very difficult to effectively identify and sustain critical capabilities—much less grow them. This was the problem facing the apparel company at the beginning of this chapter, as it tried to outsource project management skills to pursue more profitable opportunities. The business case for transferring these capabilities to an outsourcing partner was compelling, but the practical execution would be unexpectedly difficult.

Top management at this apparel company based in the Southeast faced another challenge, too. In addition to the outsourcing problem, they were pursuing an aggressive growth strategy, which called for expanding stores and product lines. But to scale operations effectively, the firm needed to add a new layer of merchandising management. Eight new divisional merchandising managers (DMMs) were needed to take over the more operational tasks previously handled by four directors of merchandising. As this international clothing retailer had grown, the directors found themselves managing teams of product managers that were too big. As a result, they had no time for increasingly important strategic activities. The DMM's role would be pivotal for the company because these new managers would be making merchandising decisions that had a direct impact on profitability—what products to buy, when, and in what quantity.

At first, this appeared to be a problem of organization design. What's the job? Where is it on the organizational chart? And how many people are needed? But company executives soon realized that defining the new role had serious talent management implications. The vice president of merchandising needed to staff the job effectively, hire the right people, and onboard and train them efficiently so all eight DMMs could be functioning quickly and consistently. This meant he needed a way to clarify and define the specific tasks and skills that new DMMs would have to master.

Working with HR, the VP's directors had already written job descriptions and used RASCI diagrams, a popular role definition tool,[5] to sort out responsibilities the new DMMs would take on. But it was not enough to clarify the actual tasks to be performed by the DMMs. For example, DMM activities such as "manage relations with vendors' senior leadership" left too much uncertainty about what hiring managers should look for in a DMM candidate and the training needed to quickly maximize the productivity of new hires. In addition, clarity around the new role's specific activities would be needed to attract top candidates.

Recognizing the problems this ambiguity posed for hiring and developing people in the new role, the firm's leaders chose to use a tool called the Skill Development Plan (SDP). Used with a facilitator, this tool provides a simple but powerful process for making explicit the specific tasks and skills required in a particular role. The SDP has been used in dozens of industries at all organizational levels to:

1. Make explicit the skills and expertise of retiring veterans to facilitate knowledge transfer
2. Clarify knowledge transfer needs for midcareer transitions such as promotions, reorganizations, or cross-training
3. Accelerate the onboarding process for new hires who can use an SDP as a road map to more quickly acquire capabilities needed to be productive[6]

The Sample Skill Development Plan shown in Table 7.1 on pages 164–65 includes about one-third of the skills that would appear in a master skill development plan for the role of senior merchandising manager in a major retailer. Before it could be used, the SDP would need to be customized for an individual. Below is an explanation of how the master SDP was developed.

The first column, "Skills and Tasks," shows a list of all the work an apprentice needs to learn how to do. Each skill is written following three rules:

1. Start with a verb.
2. Make sure you can say "go do it."
3. Make sure it can be explained in one to three hours.

The second column, "Sequence," is used to identify the individual skills that the new employee needs to learn right now, and to put them in a logical order. For instance, they might learn the skill on line 27 first and the skill on line 15 second, and so on, depending on the situation.

The third column, "Test," is used to set expectations around the three to five questions the apprentice should be able to answer before going to work using the skill. (Suggested questions are described in the key in Table 7.1.)

The fourth column, "Date," is the date by which the apprentice can answer the test questions in the third column.

The fifth column, "Resources," is used to inventory all of the documentation, training, samples, templates, and peer mentors that are available and appropriate for the apprentice to use in gathering enough information to answer the test questions.

Using the SDP framework, the merchandising directors followed a straightforward process to identify the specific tasks in column one that would be part of the divisional merchandising manager's role (see Table 7.1). For example, using a role responsibility RASCI matrix previously created, the group identified seven general areas of focus, such as vendor relationships, cross-divisional leadership, and industry leadership. Working through these areas, the directors identified tasks such as "negotiating floor space in stores," "writing business plans for specialty departments," and "representing merchandising at marketing department meetings." In about three hours, 75 tasks were listed in column one.

Then the group began reviewing the resources available to train new DMMs on these tasks, listing these in column five of the matrix. It turned out that know-how for negotiating floor space was already widely available in the company and could be taught easily. Directors also realized they were the

TABLE 7.1   Sample Skill Development Plan

Skills and Tasks	Sequence	Test*	Date	Resources
Write a specialty department business plan	1	1,2,3,7, 14	1-Mar	Joe Wilson (mentor), template (include URL), samples (include URL)
Write product communication strategy	2	1,2,3,7, 11,13	7-Mar	Martha Watson (mentor), template (include URL), samples (include URL)
Write new category development business plans	3	1,2,3,7, 8,9	12-Mar	Joe Wilson (mentor), template (include URL), samples (include URL)
Lead meeting with vendor executives				
Edit pricing philosophy document				
Present product and category trends				
Attend brand alignment meetings				
Provide input and direction on retail floor design				
Negotiate floor space within specialty shop				

Skills and Tasks	Sequence	Test*	Date	Resources
Provide input on fixture requests				
Monitor space planning and capacity of product managers				
Attend direct-mail catalog meeting				
Allocate space within the catalog				
Present direct-mail spread and theme allocation to the product managers				
Choose vendor promotions to be supported for a seasonal campaign				
Provide input on cross-functional goals				
Read cross-division president's report				
Write monthly president's report				
Read store assortment feedback				

*Key for Test (middle column)

Suggested test questions training plan

Below is a list of potential test questions that an apprentice could answer to demonstrate his or her knowledge of the skill. Of course, the apprentice will also be asked to demonstrate the skill, but these questions can be asked to show depth of tacit as well as explicit knowledge. Testing a specific skill usually requires choosing 3–5 questions.

Be able to explain:

1. The top 10 vocabulary words
2. The number of steps in the process and why each is important
3. The top three things that often go wrong
4. The relationship between X and Y (how it fits in the product cycle)
5. How to troubleshoot the three most common problems
6. The first four things to check when troubleshooting anything
7. Who is or should be involved, affected, or consulted and why
8. How to identify and define a *problem* versus a *crisis* in this area
9. How to escalate a problem or crisis in this area
10. Three best practices for this topic
11. Where to find resources (documents, people, samples, websites, etc.)
12. How to choose between X and Y
13. How quality is measured
14. What standards exist and how rigorously they are applied
15. How the skill relates to their overall job (such as how often and how important)

only ones who knew what knowledge and skills were needed to effectively represent merchandising in marketing meetings. This was knowledge they would have to pass on directly to their DMMs. They also realized it was essential that DMMs write business plans that met a certain standard, so a new template was needed for this task.

As the SDP matrix was refined throughout the first week, the third column was filled in. These were the test questions directors could use to determine when their DMMs had acquired sufficient skills to perform a task. Each task had its own set of test questions, which were easily developed from a generic list.

For example, to be judged competent in their roles, DMMs would need to be able to answer the questions: Whom do you need to contact, consult with, or inform before making this decision? What are the three most common mistakes, for example, merchandising people make in brand alignment meetings with the marketing department? What standards exist when negotiating floor space, and how rigorously are they applied?

Once the skill development plan for DMMs was developed, the apparel company was much better prepared to recruit and hire these eight new managers. The SDP also helped ensure that DMMs acquired standardized skills for key tasks like writing business plans. And management had a clear set of criteria for evaluating how new hires were doing and where they might need extra coaching. Using the skill development plan also clarified what special knowledge directors and product managers had that needed to be transferred to new DMMs. Finally, the SDP helped ensure that the firm would be able to create and sustain high levels of performance for this critical new role in the company.

There are a variety of tools, frameworks, and processes that can be used to make skills and knowledge more explicit. These can be used to define new roles, as they were at the clothing retailer, or they can be used to surface existing capabilities to make them more transferable. Regardless of the immediate objective, every executive should evaluate such investments by asking questions such as:

- How will this process or tool help us prioritize the specific skills or tasks that are most critical?
- How will this initiative help us clarify expectations for a particular role in the future?
- How will this investment reduce the ramp-up to productivity?
- How will it help me spend my talent management resources wisely?

Your staff should be able to answer these questions before you sign off on investments that promise to clarify the tasks, skills, and knowledge needed to make more effective decisions about managing talent.

Five Keys to Accelerated Leadership Development
Virtually every organization we studied is trying to accelerate the development of its young leaders. There are at least three reasons for this.

- Organizations like Cisco, GE, and New York Life that have aggressive growth plans know they can't achieve their strategic objectives without a deep pool of talented leaders.

- Many organizations went through prolonged hiring freezes and layoffs in the last 25 years, so the age distribution of their workforce is distinctly bimodal. They have lots of 50-somethings in leadership and senior technical positions, quite a few 25- to 35-year-olds in more junior roles, and a serious shortage of talent in the midcareer years. That means they must accelerate the development of junior staff much faster than in the past.[7]
- Some organizations recognize that the critical traits of successful leaders in the 21st century are different than in the past, so virtually all leaders—young and old—need updated training to succeed in the new environment.

With so many organizations focused on accelerating leadership development today—and with practices evolving so fast—it is most productive to focus on principles that will hold in the future when evaluating any new investment in this area. Here are five things that progressive firms do when trying to maximize their investments to accelerate leadership development.

1. Identify the Most Critical Leadership Roles to Be Filled in the Future

The Franciscan Health System, which includes five full-service hospitals in Washington state, has a committee of senior executives oversee its leadership development program. The committee works from the system's strategic plan when selecting candidates for the leadership development pool. Who will they need to run the new outpatient center in two years? And what leadership roles must be filled in the years ahead to grow the oncology service line? Working from the strategic plan continually focuses talent investments where they are most needed to drive the business. Do you have a way to identify the most critical roles and to fast-track candidates for those positions?

2. Assess Leadership Candidates Holistically for Their Real Potential

In addition to assessing the abilities of potential leaders, AMN Healthcare, the largest health-care staffing company in the United States, also evaluates levels of engagement and aspiration. This gives top management a much more accurate picture of the company's bench strength. That's because research by the Corporate Leadership Council shows that more than 60 percent of high performers lack the high level of engagement or the level of aspiration needed to succeed in more senior roles in their current organization.[8] Are you doing what you can to make sure you are investing leadership development resources in employees who are most likely to have a big impact on the future of the business?

3. Define Effective Leadership Behaviors for the Organization

Taking a holistic approach to evaluating future leaders doesn't mean assuming one size fits all when it comes to development, as firms like Google, P&G, and Shell have learned. "To have a monolithic view of leadership sets you up for a lot of problems," said Laszlo Bock, Google's vice president for people operations. "Having the right balance of generalists and specialists is important. Some leaders excel technically, and some stand out because they're innovative, creative thinkers. What you need is a portfolio of people with widely varying skill sets."[9]

This view is somewhat at odds with more traditional organizations like GE that still try to evaluate leaders on a relatively standard set of criteria. But, as organizations become more global and decentralized, there will be greater variation in what prove to be effective leadership characteristics. "First, top management needs to look around and ask, 'Are these the leaders we will need in three to five years to get us where we're going?'" said Jo Moore, senior vice president of Caliper, who leads her firm's practice consulting with top management teams. "Almost always the answer is 'No.' Then you need to build competency models of what leadership skills are needed to get you there."

Shell's activities in China show how one company has recognized evolving needs in different markets. Given the difficulty of retaining high-potential talent in that rapidly growing market, Shell identified career stewards who meet with young leaders continually to help them set realistic career expectations, make sure they get access to the best development opportunities, and monitor their level of engagement.[10] Does the leadership competency model your organization uses, or whatever behaviors you want to promote, fit the demands of your business strategy and the changing markets in which you operate?

4. Create High-Impact Leadership Development Opportunities

To accelerate development of new capabilities, young leaders need to be consulted on strategic issues sooner and top management needs to watch closely what they do with that opportunity. Creating accelerated talent pools and assigning them special projects has become pretty common practice to see which high-potential candidates really stand out. Firms that are more effective in this practice consistently involve top management in the process of identifying and monitoring the development of high potentials. It's still too easy for promising talent to be hidden by business unit and functional managers, when they really should be considered a corporate asset. Johnson & Johnson's LeAD program is designed to break this barrier with a nine-month program that gives future leaders intensive coaching, exposure in emerging markets such as China and Brazil, and higher levels of visibility to senior management across the corporation.[11]

P&G takes an even more aggressive approach to accelerate leadership development. One major division has identified difficult, high-impact "crucible roles" as a chance to test out high potentials. Roles such as "director of marketing for a new region" or "brand manager for a leading product" are now more likely to be filled by qualified high potentials. Top management's philosophy is that meaningful development takes place best in "live fire" roles when future leaders are tested under conditions of real stress.[12] Are your best and brightest truly visible to leadership at the top of the organization? And are you doing whatever you can to get them the types of developmental assignments they need to lead the firm into the future?

5. Get Fast Feedback on the Performance of Future Leaders

Organizations that are best at accelerating development create processes or tools to provide top management with quick, interim feedback to show how candidates are faring. Faster development often means giving high potentials more challenging or riskier assignments. To maximize learning, minimize damage from mistakes, and more quickly identify those who won't make it, smart executives find ways to shrink the feedback loop on the performance of young leaders. For example, the COO in a United Kingdom–based global consumer products company was concerned about how his new country general managers were developing. So he had a simple tool created that could track the progress of new GMs at three-month intervals. A series of performance criteria that were easily observed, such as "being visible in the business" or "contributes to the above-market team," allowed the COO to compare the progress of 15 new GMs across regions. It also gave him early feedback on who needed help and who might not succeed in their new positions. Do you have ways of quickly evaluating whether your approaches to leadership development are paying off and what changes must be made to maximize learning?

The shortage of midcareer leadership talent combined with the need for more sophisticated executives who can run complex, distributed, fast-changing organizations means that accelerating leadership development will become an essential capability for firms in the years ahead. When assessing initiatives in this area, consider how they (1) focus resources on critical roles; (2) assess leadership candidates holistically; (3) define and support the leadership behaviors needed in a diverse organization; (4) create more dramatic and appealing learning opportunities; and (5) make faster midcourse corrections in the learning process by shortening the performance feedback loop.

More Innovative Solutions Required

Economic volatility in recent years has taken some of the pressure off organizations to invest heavily in recruiting, developing, and retaining talent. Older employees and executives are staying on the job longer due to new uncertainties about the value of their retirement assets. Younger workers have changed jobs less often because opportunities have been limited and the risks of getting caught without a seat in a game of employment musical chairs has been too great.

However, many surveys have shown there is tremendous pent up demand in the workforce to pursue new job opportunities when available. In a way, the last recession gave HR a respite and has allowed firms to skate by with some pretty unimaginative talent-related initiatives. Certainly, some of this is due to a lack of support and resources from top management. But going forward, if you are a leader in an organization where talent really counts, you must expect your staff to come up with more innovative solutions. The examples in Chapters 6 and 7 are an attempt to raise awareness in terms of what you should be looking for. Now we turn to one of the most vexing problems when it comes to managing talent: measurement. None of the solutions proposed here would have gone anywhere if executive sponsors had not held their staff accountable for results, which is the focus of Chapter 8.

For Talent Management and HR Business Partners

Presenting Talent Management Innovations to Executives

Chapters 6 and 7 present numerous different approaches to managing talent. When you're discussing these new ideas with business executives, avoid buzzwords. For example, don't get caught up in explaining the nuances conducting an "employee engagement survey" versus an "employee satisfaction sur-

(continued)

vey." Instead, when speaking with business executives, keep the focus on the business goals the talent management solution aims to advance.

To establish the efficacy and credibility of new ideas in a line executive's mind, for any proposed solution, be ready to:

- State the business problem in plain language
- State the cost (or potential cost) of the problem
- Share data—research, or even anecdotal reports—to prove your point
- Describe existing solutions and tell why they are inadequate
- Describe your proposed solutions in plain language
- Tell who would be affected and who would have to participate in the solution
- Tell how long the solution will take to implement and what it would cost
- Describe how results would be measured

When presenting to executives, it's important to think about all of these issues from their perspective. For example, you would probably adopt a different style when presenting to a CEO who came up through finance and values hard data as opposed to a CEO who came up through marketing and might be more interested in stories and examples. You should always prepare an in-depth analysis of the points listed here, as well as a short executive summary.

In addition, you should be able to answer the questions listed in Chapter 6's comment, "For Talent Management and HR Business Partners: Keeping Up with Innovations in Talent Management."

8

Creating Measures That Matter in Talent Management

Every year millions are spent on initiatives to improve leadership development, mentoring, onboarding, employee engagement, and performance management. Unfortunately, in many organizations, the benefits of these efforts are suspect, unknown, or nonexistent. This is, in large part, due to executive sponsors not knowing what they really want from these programs and neglecting to require follow-up reports about the benefits. In some cases, we find that leaders just don't care about measurement. They believe that some investments in talent management are so fundamental they don't need to be measured.

Often, the lack of useful metrics in talent management is due to three issues. The first issue is the erroneous assumption that measures have to be exact numbers to be valuable. Second, leaders often assume that measuring talent management effectiveness is impossible because concepts like onboarding, leadership development, and mentoring seem so abstract. Finally, quantitative information and analysis is often focused exclusively on routine HR activities, for example, cost per hire, that add little value in executive decision making.[1] Ironically, in riskier situations with a greater range of outcomes, leaders are more likely to ignore the value of measurement and rely on intuition.

But effective leaders can avoid these mistakes by making a more thorough connection between talent management activities and business results. To measure the effectiveness of talent management, executives must examine how effectively (or not) they are managing talent risks and seizing talent opportunities. They must avoid the temptation to rely only on obvious measures of the performance of HR. As we have been saying throughout this book, when executives think about talent management, they must think clearly. It is surprisingly straightforward to do this: Think about what you want, and then measure whether or not you get it. Continually ask, How is talent management advancing business strategy?

This means, for example, that you should care less about the number of employees who are hired in a given time frame and, instead, be concerned with information that shows whether or not these new employees are quickly productive and working on important tasks. You're not as interested in how many managers attended a leadership workshop, but you do want to know what percentage of your managers gives regular performance feedback and holds employees accountable for clear results. And you're not only interested in how many people are on the "high performers" list. You also want to know whether these high performers see a clear future for themselves in your company.

It can seem difficult to access this information, so the temptation is to measure what's easy when you look at talent management. After all, it's straightforward to report how many people attended a training seminar. It's far more difficult to determine that the training was successful—that is, did the quality of work improve? It's satisfying to report that you have a succession planning process in place, but it's more important to know that you could have an executive-level successor prepared when it's time to take over. This kind of broad, results-focused measurement is central to developing and sustaining an effective talent management strategy.

Based on recent research and our experience, we believe three practices are essential for executives who want to use measurement more effectively in making talent-related decisions.[2]

1. **Focus on outcomes.** Clarify what outcome you expect to achieve, and design measurements to evaluate progress toward that outcome.
2. **Go beyond hard data.** Incorporate different types of measurement into your data gathering and analysis.
3. **Champion measurement.** Continually follow through on the implications of information you receive. Make it clear that measures matter.

Focus on Outcomes

An effective system of talent management measures can only come from a deep, logical connection between talent and organizational success. Once this framework is created, then the measures linking talent and business outcomes become self-evident.[3]

- **Insist on measures that reflect business outcomes, not just talent management activities.** John Boudreau and Peter Ramstad like to point out that the accounting department provides information about overall business performance, not just about the performance of the accounting department itself.[4] Similarly, your talent management staff should be providing information about business performance—not merely measuring HR's efficiency.

- **Ask questions that define outcomes.** When an outcome appears immeasurable, ask questions that force your staff to define that outcome specifically. When you increase understanding of the goal of a talent management activity, you make it easier to evaluate the success or failure of that activity.

- **Target key opportunities and risks for measurement.** Resist the tendency to shoot from the hip when a situation is amorphous and changing. Aspects of even the most seemingly unpredictable scenarios can be quantified. If you're implementing a measurement program, make sure the data collected relates to your most important challenges.

- **Use measures that can influence specific decisions.** Make sure everything you're measuring can be analyzed and supports an important decision. Measures that have no effect on decisions or predictions have no value.[5]

Measure Business Outcomes—Not Talent Management Activities

In many situations, the greatest value of metrics comes from demonstrating links between talent resources and business outcomes. For example, say our strategy is to expand sales in minority markets. To succeed we need more members of minorities in sales. To evaluate the success of our talent management efforts, we would ask what percentage of our new salespeople meet our diversity criteria. We are more interested in this actual percentage than in asking how many job fairs for minority professionals the recruiters have attended, for example. And eventually, of course, we want to know how our sales improve in the targeted markets due to the number of new salespeople meeting our diversity criteria.

Most measures generated by HR departments today, such as job fairs attended, report how HR and talent management functions are employing resources, and how efficiently these resources are being used,[6] but they fail to take the next step and make an explicit connection to business objectives. If measures are to help talent management improve organizational performance, they must be developed from a more holistic, business-oriented perspective.

At the very least, when asked to support specific talent initiatives, executives should be asking, What business outcomes are we trying to influence? For example, how will this investment in improving succession planning reduce uncertainty in the capital markets? Or increase customer satisfaction? Or increase productivity?

"Of course, the specific measures that matter depend on the company," says Jonathan Low, a partner in Predictiv Consulting, experts on intangibles measurement. "But an executive needs to look at what are the outcomes that drive decisions around capital market perceptions, employment market perceptions, and customer perceptions. In other words, how do talent management investments influence outcomes in these areas that ultimately drive business performance?"[7]

It can be difficult to make explicit links between business outcomes and talent investments because so many variables play a role. But you can learn a great deal by listening to the way sponsors of talent investments talk about, and think about, this connection. For example, in response to your query about investing in a succession planning program, the following explanation would be right on target: "In our industry, analysts have been expressing concerns about the strength of our executive bench and its impact on our ability to execute our strategy versus our two major competitors. So investing in succession planning will directly address the question analysts have about us. For every senior leadership position, this program is expected to help us identify two leaders who have been trained and are prepared to take over."

Stating *specifically* what you want to achieve is the essential starting point of measurement. In practice, this means you must define the change you seek. For example, as described in Chapter 7, a major retailer is adding a level of management in its merchandising department to handle growth. To measure the eventual result of adding eight new management positions, the retailer needs to state clearly its expectations: What is a highly functioning merchandising manager? What tasks will these managers take on? What decisions will they be able to make? What numbers will they be responsible for affecting? What relationships will they have built? What will this new layer of management mean for the productivity of those people currently a level up and a level down? How will the retailer know it has hired the right people? Six months down the line, what does the sponsoring executive want to see?

Douglas Hubbard, a leading authority on measuring intangibles,[8] shows the importance of defining your terms. For example, what do you mean by "a good succession plan"? Do you mean that different areas of your company are coordinating succession planning so people aren't double- or triple-counted? Do you mean that you are finding opportunities for people both inside and outside their current departments? Do you mean that cross-company promotion is a priority? Define the specific, observable changes you seek.

Ask Questions to Define Your Measures

Executives who want their staff to develop more useful measurements to improve the evaluation of talent management investments should challenge colleagues with questions based on two assumptions:[9]

1. If something *seems* immeasurable, it is almost always only perceived as such because no one has carefully defined the concept to be measured.
2. If you can't detect a change in something, it's not worth investing in.

When subordinates argue that something is important, but claims are made that it cannot be measured (or when proposed measurements seem inadequate), use the following line of reasoning to help colleagues create measures that make sense. We'll use "mentoring" as an example of a talent-related investment. It's an area where inadequate measures have created great frustration for executives over the years.

Start the process with this question: If you are saying we need to invest in this mentoring program, what exactly do *you* mean by "mentoring"? You may have to ask that question several times in order to clarify what mentoring means in your organization. Then follow this logic:

- If mentoring (or some other initiative) is something we care about, then the results of mentoring must be detectable or observable in some way. (We wouldn't care about mentoring if it was completely undetectable—directly or indirectly.) In other words, if this proposed program is successful, what will we be able to observe or detect that is different in the organization? For example, people who have been mentored will show a measurable improvement in 10 specific skills. Or, maybe they'll be able to list 10 new relationships within the company and note how those new contacts help them do their jobs.

- If mentoring is detectable, then it can be detected as some amount. In other words, we can observe, more or less, the result of mentoring: new engineers reaching full productivity in four months instead of six, for example, or product managers who present their marketing plans in a consistent way. Evaluating the effect of any talent management initiative begins with clearly identifying the object of measurement and how it can be detected.

There are two ways you can coach yourself or others through the process of figuring out what measureable results you want to observe or detect. One simple way is to picture people or processes that are working on target and then describe any observable aspects of this scenario. For example, if one of your most effective managers conducts regular one-on-one sessions and asks for weekly written status reports, you may use that behavior as a model for others. Then you could track and measure the effects of these behaviors on productivity, quality, and employee engagement.

The second way you can figure out the results you are looking for is to picture people or processes that are failing and examine what is *not* working. Often it is easier to make a list of what you don't like than what you do. For example, you may find it very frustrating that presentations given by less experienced managers do not seem to be rooted in a deep understanding of the business strategy. You can then track and measure their ability to answer the big picture questions in Chapter 3 as a way to mitigate that problem.

Insist on Measurement When Risks and Costs Are Highest

Creating and analyzing measures should focus on helping leaders make difficult decisions where risks and/or costs of failure are greatest. When you decide how to use data and qualitative information to reduce uncertainty, ask yourself, Where are bad decisions most likely to produce serious and negative outcomes? In other words, what are the high-impact decisions? For those decisions, what information could increase your chances of taking the right action?

Hubbard, in his ongoing work on measurement, reports being continually surprised by what he calls the "risk paradox." He has found a consistent pattern where organizations that use any quantitative risk analysis tend to do so only for routine operational decisions. Meanwhile, major, relatively high-risk decisions get virtually no attention in applying measures to reduce uncertainty.[10] Top managers can gain a significant advantage if they approach talent management by identifying decisions they must make that pose the greatest uncertainty and the greatest potential costs if they are wrong. This is where measurement, even in its most limited forms, will pay the biggest dividends. Talent management experts Boudreau and Ramstad note, "Even imperfect measures aimed at the right areas may be more illuminating than very elegant measures aimed at the wrong place. . . . Ultimately, measurement systems are only as valuable as the decisions they improve."[11]

For example, the new CEO of the United Kingdom–based consumer products company described in Chapter 1 planned to implement an aggressive strategy to turn his decentralized multinational business into an integrated global enterprise. Even though the firm had an elaborate talent management infrastructure, the CEO recognized a major risk since the company did not actually have a pipeline of leadership talent robust enough to support the planned expansion. If he went ahead with the strategy without adequate leadership talent, the effort would fail, costing the company millions.

To address this uncertainty, the head of HR oversaw a detailed analysis of the company's global succession pipeline for the top 200 leadership positions. The analysis applied a strict 1-1-2 formula for every top management position: there had to be one named successor being developed to fill the role in the short term and two additional candidates specifically identified as potential successors in the long term. The analysis clearly showed that the talent pool at the business unit level was inadequate and posed an unacceptable risk that would undermine the firm's new business strategy. In this situation, having information that was gathered in a structured way—the 1-1-2 formula—played a critical role in reducing uncertainty about talent-related risks, allowing the CEO to take immediate corrective action and avoid making an unsupported strategic bet.

A common high-stakes decision involving talent is succession planning for the CEO or other critical C-level roles. According to a recent study, 39 percent of CEOs and board directors reported that they had "zero" viable internal candidates to succeed the chief executive.[12] Companies like Merrill-Lynch and Bank of America have learned the high cost for shareholders if the uncertainties of CEO succession are not addressed.[13] In contrast, Procter & Gamble provides one of the best examples of succession risk that is monitored with metrics to reduce uncertainty around C-level succession. P&G has 10 criteria on which it evaluates potential CEO successors.[14]

The loss of critical knowledge due to turnover of technical and professional staff is another example of potentially costly talent-related risks that can be mitigated with better use of measures. In Chapter 4, we showed how the chief executive at a power generating station identified the risks he faced with the looming retirement of dozens of veteran engineers in the plant. Knowing which retirements would have the most serious impact reduced uncertainty. By getting a quantitative handle on the risks of retirements, plant leaders were able to make well-informed decisions about where to concentrate resources to accelerate knowledge transfer—and, thus, better manage the risks they were facing.

To have a real impact on business performance, measures must reflect an understanding of the nuances of an organization's current workforce and where differences in the performance of a specific role pose the greatest risk for the organization.[15] A simple way to start identifying these performance differences, which need to be measured, is to ask, Where would a change in the availability or quality of talent have the greatest impact on the success of our organization? The answer to this question starts to define your "pivotal talent pools," which Cascio and Boudreau illustrate this way:

At Xilinx, the world's largest manufacturer of programmable logic chips, the ability to innovate, to develop new products, is key to the firm's success in the marketplace. A pivotal talent pool is, therefore, engineers, for as [now retired] CEO Wim Roelandts is fond of saying, "De-motivated engineers don't create breakthrough products."[16]

Similarly, Daimler Trucks North America was concerned about the threat of losing specialized technical skills and customer knowledge used to build its highly customized trucks. Leaders knew that up to 50 percent of the division's workforce in some functions would be eligible to retire in the next few years. To identify specific capabilities at risk, the company surveyed 5,000 employees to understand the types of knowledge that could be lost. This study showed that across the firm, about 20 percent of employees were classified as "key knowledge holders," 9 percent as "unique key knowledge holders," and 3 percent as "at-risk, unique knowledge holders." This latter group was defined as employees eligible to retire within five years.[17] Reducing uncertainty about where its capabilities were at risk was an essential step in deciding where to invest talent management resources.

Use Measures That Will Influence Specific Decisions

In talent management, data is needed to analyze different types of decisions. Measures are used to:

- **Diagnose specific threats.** Is this risk serious? For example, what percentage of our top 200 executives has successors ready to step in?
- **Evaluate proposed solutions.** Should we invest in this option? For example, what are the costs of hiring and training nurses from foreign markets?
- **Support implementation and drive organizational change.** Are we developing the new behaviors we need? For example, what percentage of managers completed their performance reviews by the deadline?
- **Evaluate progress and impacts of major talent initiatives or specific local programs.** Is this investment delivering

what was needed? For example, how many interns from last year's program were hired as full-time employees?

If you believe that you are vulnerable in a particular talent area, for example, leadership pipeline, onboarding new hires, or retention of midcareer employees, your talent management focus should be on gathering information to support decisions in these areas.[18] When deciding what metrics are needed or when evaluating existing data, you should first ask, What decisions are these measurements supposed to support? For example, the CEO of New York Life Insurance recognized he needed to accelerate the development of more sophisticated decision-making skills among high-potential talent. Once several initiatives were launched, the chief executive and his staff would have to continually evaluate whether the firm was making adequate progress developing this more junior talent. Thus, the measurement system had to collect data that made it possible for top management to assess the quality of the leadership pipeline and, as a result, make appropriate decisions. This link between decisions and measures may seem obvious, but it is remarkable how often organizations create metrics that have zero influence on any decision making. The clear implication, says Hubbard, is that measurements that do not influence decision making have no value.[19]

In practice, this means that if you have a couple of hours a month to devote to talent management and your company has 75 programs, you can only track the 2 to 4 most important ones. For a large health-care company, for example, succession planning is number one. Its executives spend 90 minutes per month tracking and talking about succession planning. In our consulting experience, most executives have not identified their top talent management activities. Those who do choose priorities have found a way to make a difference, despite limited time.

Go Beyond Hard Data

There is widespread misunderstanding in organizations about the definition and purpose of "measurement." The standard dictionary definition of *measurement* is "the size, amount, or degree of something." This implies a number, but metrics need not be an exact number to be useful. Experts contend that managers have become much too fixated on the idea that quantitative measures must be overly precise.

"The commonplace notion that presumes measures are exact quantities ignores the usefulness of simply reducing uncertainty," says Hubbard.[20] He argues that, according to scientific methods, simply reducing uncertainty, rather than eliminating it, is the real objective of measurement.

For talent management, anecdotal evidence (stories); the hard data provided by financial, HR, and operational systems; and managers' observations all can be useful. All kinds of information, thoughtfully collected, can reduce uncertainty. For example, AMN Healthcare identified through interviews that a certain percentage of its top 200 young leaders had no aspirations to move into senior roles. Collecting this data gave AMN more information about its bench strength and helped the firm identify who its real high potentials were. This analysis helped AMN focus on its most likely prospects so the company was able to earn a better return on its investments in leadership development.[21] When we think of measurement as the process of obtaining information that reduces uncertainty, it changes our ideas about what metrics can add value in talent management. The realm of possibilities expands considerably.

Many of your staff members are likely to have limited ideas about what measurements are or can be. By only focusing on trying to define the amount or degree of something, staff members can miss many opportunities for adding value to the process of managing talent. Engage your staff in a discussion about the definition and meaning of measurement in order to bring more qualitative factors into the mix and to allow for some fuzziness in the numbers. The key is that the measures you invest in help reduce uncertainty about critical risks and support specific decisions.

Look Beyond Financial Data for Valuable Measures

Steve Carlson, CEO of Community Medical Center in Missoula, Montana, explained how the fuzzy math of talent management can make it difficult to justify important investments: "It's so much easier to spend $600,000 on a new CAT scan machine, as opposed to spending $100,000 on a new assistant manager one year *before* the head of the department retires. For many executives, it's all about managing the labor dollars and keeping them to the absolute minimum. But we don't really know the opportunity costs, plus hard dollar losses, when we have a difficult leadership transition."

Although it can be hard to pin down the value of that $100,000 expense in terms of mistakes avoided and opportunities seized, this soft opportunity cost could be as critical to an organization's success as the $600,000 investment in new equipment. However, since the value of the talent management investment is difficult to predict—and the costs of not investing in training of the new manager may not be obvious—it can be very difficult to justify the training expense. Another hospital president articulated the dilemma, saying, "The problem is the lack of clarity that's related to the ROI. The risk/return is much more nebulous in pipeline management, so it tends to get pushed off." This situation is what you want to avoid: ignoring a seriously important risk to your organization just because it cannot be stated in hard financial terms.

The Knowledge Silo Matrix (KSM) is an example of a measurement tool that gathers valuable nonfinancial information. Managers in the power plant described in Chapter 4 interviewed employees using the KSM to identify 350 discrete knowledge domains—creating a wealth of actionable information. Observations also identified which silos had one or more mentors available to transfer knowledge. The evaluation also showed how many apprentices were available, if any, to develop essential capabilities in each knowledge silo. The outputs from the KSM, while not financial data, are quantitative information that reduced uncertainty and supported important management decisions, such as:

- Which critical capabilities are most at risk if we don't invest further resources in transferring knowledge to junior staff?
- Which expert mentors are most overextended in training others and, therefore, need additional support so they don't leave prematurely?
- Which skill areas have redundant expertise that might be redeployed elsewhere?

The Knowledge Silo Matrix is an example of a different way to measure nonfinancial information that provides insights to influence decisions made by managers at a certain level in the organization. While the KSM would not necessarily produce data used by senior leaders, it illustrates the essential connection you should require between measurement systems and the talent-related decisions you must make. If the information you are getting does not support decisions you are responsible for, then look for ways to find information that is helpful.

Look Beyond HR-Centric Measures

The proliferation of IT-based HR systems means that businesses have access to a steady stream of scorecards and dashboards that focus on the efficiency and effectiveness of HR programs,[22] instead of on how HR programs actually affect the business. Measures today are readily available for things like the following:

- Costs of providing HR services, for example, cost per hire, training costs
- Satisfaction of the workforce with HR programs
- Cost of outsourced HR activities
- Hours of training received by new employees in the first year
- Sick days per employee per year
- Percentage of turnover and turnover costs
- Recruiting, for example, how many open positions, how many candidates interviewed, how many positions filled this week
- Number of attendees (total number or percentage of population) in a training program and their reaction via exit survey
- For technology solutions, number of unique users, posts, or time logged in
- Number of candidates in the high-potential pool

The dashboard concept is a routine part of the executive's tool kit, and many of these metrics are useful for decision making in certain contexts. Executives certainly want some of this information as a quick check on the status of talent management, and HR needs these measures to evaluate projects at a detailed level.

But this HR data is not enough. These IT-generated HR-centric measures encourage a narrow view of measurement. Senior executives who must evaluate major talent risks, talent investments, and the effects of these initiatives on business performance and organizational capabilities need to be able to look more broadly at the impact of talent management on business performance. The executive's challenge is not only to evaluate the efficiency of talent management activities but also to assess progress toward a more qualitative goal: a workforce and leadership team ready to implement your business strategy over the next three to five years.

Champion Measurement

It's likely that at the inception of almost every project, you ask for measures of ROI, improvement, and effectiveness. You want to know how you'll measure success before you invest money in a talent management activity. It's equally likely that at the end of those same projects, these numbers have not been tracked. Measurement frequently gets dropped in the face of day-to-day business pressures. But measurement is key to improving performance. That's why leaders must champion measurement in four ways:

- Follow up. If you believe a business outcome is important, regularly ask about measures of that outcome.
- Explain why measurement is important. Make sure your commitment is clear.

- Expect all levels of management to measure outcomes and act on what they learn.
- Look for metrics that show long-term benefits, not just the short-term data that is easiest to obtain.

Follow Up to Maximize the Value of Measurement

If your measures are truly important for driving performance, keep asking about them, again and again. The CEO of the consumer products company discussed earlier in the chapter discovered his 1-1-2 analysis of the firm's global succession pipeline showed a serious deficiency threatening the business strategy. Collaborating with his global director of HR, this chief executive immediately launched an initiative to make sustainable succession planning a key business imperative for all the company's executives. As a result, all general managers of large business units were given a 1-1-2 succession planning target. This meant that executives were evaluated on whether they were successfully developing one short-term successor and two potential long-term successors for all roles on their local leadership team. The 1-1-2 talent measure is now assessed regularly by local and regional executive teams, as well as by corporate committees. "The key was hard wiring these succession health checks into clear objectives for our leaders," said one senior manager.

The point is don't waste a good measure by failing to keep the organization's attention focused on it. Change starts with overcoming inertia, a force we cannot overestimate, and in our experience, regular check-ins are *the* way to do so. Check in or ask for status before you start the project, after approval, during the project, and at the end. Include checkup points throughout the implementation. For example, if one month after a training class, participants are "too busy" to implement what they learned, the program isn't going to deliver results.

Your staff needs to know you're serious when you do this. Make a formal assessment schedule. Decide when you want to follow up and put it in your calendar. It's one thing to tell managers you are going to start monitoring on-time completion of employees' performance reviews, an activity clearly linked to employee satisfaction. But it's quite another to withhold their bonuses when they miss the deadline. That's what the president of one major hospital system did. At first, only 73 percent of the hospital's managers finished on time. Since bonuses, representing 10 percent of a manager's salary, were withheld, however, that number has jumped to 97 percent.

There is considerable debate about the use of positive and negative sanctions in situations like this. Research shows positive rewards are definitely the preferred route.[23] Your organization's culture will dictate what will work best. But sometimes the system needs a little jolt, especially when you are trying to get managers to pay attention to a critical new measure.

Promote the Value of Measurement

An essential part of top management's job is communicating the logic between talent investments and business performance to the rest of the organization. That's because, until the relationships between talent and the business become part of the culture and the dominant logic of management, the effects of measures will remain limited. One senior executive in a major consumer products company demonstrated this logic, saying, "Our guys get the risks. It's so clear to them that if we don't have a sustainable talent pipeline, then you lose profits because key roles aren't filled with the right people and people underperform."

You must make time to sell the importance of your key measures to your management team. The implications for a measure may be painfully obvious to you, but that doesn't mean your colleagues understand it. Vestas Wind Systems is an energy provider based in Denmark. Its North American headquarters in Portland, Oregon, was undergoing explosive growth a few years ago when Vestas, then a company of 14,000, had to onboard 8,000 new employees in a single year. Predictably, turnover rates among new hires became a major problem, and top management wanted to expand onboarding initiatives to include considerably more training. The senior vice president responsible, however, knew she had to sell managers on the idea of delaying the start of the new hires for added training. Although the program would ultimately reduce turnover, line managers wanted their new employees on the job now! The SVP created a financial model showing that the turnover costs of one bad hire was equal to a year's salary. Instead of simply sharing these measures with colleagues in a report or an e-mail, this executive went on the road, visiting managers across the company. She put her numbers in front of them and made her case face-to-face, showing how much money the company would save if managers supported the new onboarding program.[24]

Even valuable measures don't sell themselves. You will often have to make a conscious effort to communicate the importance of talent-related metrics in order to change behaviors and decision making in the organization. This means presenting measures and an analysis that matches existing mental models of your managers when it comes to talent management. Experts have found that it often works best to start by sharing relatively simple measures and analyses. For example, turnover cost analysis often proves to be the first evidence many managers have seen that demonstrates the business value of measures relating to managing talent.[25] So plan to spend some time explaining the value of important new measures, and calibrate the complexity of your presentation to your audience.

Expect All Managers to Measure

In practice, you want to be sure measurement and evaluation are occurring at all levels. Talk to the people affected by your top-priority talent management efforts. Shake hands with interns and ask about their experiences. Drop in on supervisor training. Talk to people in the high-potential pool and get a sense of how they see the future. Ask apprentices in the mentor program to tell you what they've learned.

Expect feedback from the sponsor of every talent management program, as well as from participants. Most important, figure out how you can learn if employees are changing behaviors as a result of a training course. Don't just ask training managers how a program went, of course. Ask a reasonable sample of participants what they're going to do as a result of the session. It shows that you're paying attention and you want to hear about results.

Look to Long-Term Benefits

If possible, set up measures that reflect the longer-term benefits of your talent management initiative. These measures may not be practical in the early stages, or even early years, of a program. But finding ways to track the long-term benefits of an investment will help leaders make the right decisions when business strategies shift and revenues inevitably slow down. For example, Microsoft has a long-running internship program, described in Chapter 6. The company tracks the long-term job performance of interns who eventually become full-time employees. This allows Microsoft to evaluate the contribution of employees hired after being interns against those hired through other channels. The former interns have consistently outperformed their colleagues in these evaluations over the years, further validating the company's investment in the program.

Another example of an organization using measures to show long-term benefits is Pitt County Memorial Hospital. Its program to retain older nurses, also described in Chapter 6, has continually monitored the careers of program participants to access the long-term retention value of this investment. The long-term retention rate of more than 97 percent helped convince top management to expand the program several years ago, despite cost-cutting pressures brought on by the recession. A lesson from these organizations is that measures valuable for assessing talent-related investments can change over time. The early stages of a program may be judged by some measures that become less important when the value of longer-term tests becomes relevant for decision making.

Measurement Must Lead to Action

Having valuable measures about the right risks in time to take action is wasted effort unless you take the right steps next. Leaders need to close the loop from measuring to decision making to get a payoff from their talent management measures.

Effective measurement will be a critical success factor in your efforts to lead change around talent management. What's the executive's job in measurement? Your job is to be clear about what you want, get agreement on how progress will be tracked and evaluated toward your vision, and then follow through with feedback on the resulting data. Chapter 9 focuses on the other key responsibilities senior executives have when it comes to driving change in this arena.

For Talent Management and HR Business Partners

Showing the Value of Talent Management

Talent management programs are a strategic investment in employees, and you should be able to measure or describe a return. Some executives find it difficult to see the value because every return on a talent management investment is not necessarily a number. That's why HR and talent management professionals need to take charge of the conversation about measurement.

Here's what you can do to help line executives see the contributions and value in this area:

- **Measure what's important to the business.** Offer measurements based on your understanding of the big picture. You could ask, "Would you rather focus on the reports we have on the productivity of recent hires (because of a backlog of work), or their employee engagement data (because we're worried about losing them to a competitor during their first 90 days on the job)?" If succession planning is important to your business, you could ask

whether they'd rather see a complete list of the identified successors for the top 100 positions cross-tabbed
to monitor for redundancy, the current list of promotions
and expected promotions, or a summary of themes from
exit interviews for high potentials who have already left
the company. By providing a variety of measures that get
at different business issues, you can help line managers
learn how to focus on what matters most.

- **Establish a baseline.** Help executives identify the highest priority talent management issues and then clearly
  define "current state." You won't know if you've made
  measurable progress if you don't have a common understanding of the issue from the start.

- **Clearly state the goals of every talent management initiative.** Look for ways to link talent management numbers
  to business-wide performance measures. For example,
  after flight attendants attend stress-reduction workshops
  (a talent management metric), do negative interactions
  with passengers decrease (an operations metric)? When
  senior engineers mentor newcomers (a talent management metric), are they able to work independently in a
  shorter time frame (a productivity metric)? If the "high
  performers list" has 100 names (a talent management
  metric), are critical senior roles filled faster (a management metric)?

- **Define measures of success up front.** Never submit a
  proposal or accept an assignment to lead a talent management activity without first agreeing on how you will
  measure success. Discuss not only the data you will
  gather—hard numbers and qualitative assessments—

(continued)

but also who is going to gather it, how it will be presented, when it will be presented, and to whom. This is a discipline that often is forgotten in the rush to execute a project.

- **Know your numbers, but don't limit yourself to financial reporting. Use stories, too.** Be prepared to show a clear link between money and time spent on the one hand and value to the business on the other. But don't get lost trying to provide a hard dollar return when anecdotal evidence can be more informative and more powerful in moving people to action.[26] Sometimes individual stories can represent the situation better than hard data. For example, it is relatively easy to chart the number of open headcount filled in a given quarter. More interesting to leaders is the relative quality, stability, and productivity of recent hires. In this example, talent management staff should be able to name recent hires whose experience represents the good and the bad of their peers, so that when you tell their story, it resonates for their managers. This includes your efforts to bring the recent hires on board, the handoff to their respective teams, and the follow-up in their first 3 to 12 months.

- **Edit your data.** Assess what measures are of interest internally to evaluate HR efficiency and effectiveness. Don't burden business managers with data that is only important to HR. For the data that you track, ask, "Who really cares?" If business managers aren't monitoring the data you present, figure out what they do want to see.

- **Resist the temptation to present only positive results.** Use measures and anecdotal evidence to give executives feedback on their involvement in the projects they are sponsoring. Deliver bad news early, so projects can be turned around. For example, if the experience of summer interns early in the summer is not positive, use that evidence to communicate concerns. Then, executives have the information they need to improve their management of the interns and follow through on their commitment as sponsor.

- **Measure progress at every stage of the employee life cycle.** For hiring, what do you measure besides the number of résumés processed, the number of candidates interviewed, and the number of positions filled? For onboarding, what do you track? For employee development, what do you measure beyond hours of training per employee or exit surveys? For retention, what do you know beyond turnover numbers? Be sure that for each stage in the employee life cycle you can articulate the risks and give a clear picture of the current state and your goals. Then you can measure and show improvement.

- **Look ahead.** Keep track of the business decisions that are on the 6- to 12-month horizon and look for how those choices will affect talent management. Then, think about ways to measure and track data that will support those decisions. For example, if you anticipate a new product launch, how will you backfill the positions left open when the new product team is formed? Look at past launches to estimate how many positions will be needed, where these people are likely to come from, and issues that came up in the teams they left behind. Then, you can present a snapshot of the future talent management issues and suggest solutions.

9

Sponsorship, Urgency, and Integration

The Executive's Role in Producing Results

It's one thing, given your business strategy, to identify talent management needs and to find creative solutions. But successfully implementing new talent initiatives is more challenging. Most operational tasks of rolling out talent-related programs or broader processes will fall to the HR talent management staff or middle management, but executives have an essential role to play. Consider these scenarios:

- The CEO of New York Life needs to implement major cultural changes to support his business growth objectives. These changes will include accelerating leadership development and creating career management programs that will help retain more junior high-potential staff who might otherwise leave. What is the CEO's role in making these changes happen?
- Health Partners, a Minnesota-based health system, has been investing in a variety of talent management initiatives for more than a decade. It started by focus-

ing on executive succession planning and then shifted attention to a few other critical areas. What would company executives have to do to drive a more broad-based talent strategy that engages leaders at all levels of the organization?

- The executive team of Coaxis, a $20 million software company, was no longer satisfied with its low profile and moderate growth, despite its consistent profitability. How could the firm's COO change its approach to staffing from the most senior levels to the front lines to support its new growth strategy?

For too many organizations, 75 percent of the energy in talent management goes into the design and creation of initiatives and only 25 percent into implementation. That's why talent-related investments are subject to the same fate as other performance improvement initiatives. Change management guru John Kotter has consistently reported that 70 percent of major change efforts either never get fully started, fail completely, or are implemented late and over budget.[1] Other researchers have reported similarly low success rates in recent years.[2]

Talent management initiatives that produce meaningful results always require significant behavior change. Examples might include:

- Supervisors and managers are required to conduct more thorough performance reviews.
- Hiring managers must ensure that everyone on the interview loop is trained to conduct interviews.
- Managers and executives must participate in regular succession planning meetings.

- Managers must put poor performers on performance improvement plans rather than shuffle them to other parts of the organization.
- High potentials are more routinely transferred to other parts of the organization on developmental assignments.
- Employees are expected to regularly identify needed skills and describe how they will attain them.

Successfully implementing and sustaining these new behaviors requires careful planning and attention from leadership throughout the change process. To succeed at overseeing the implementation of talent initiatives, leaders, of course, have a role to play in standard change activities, such as clearly communicating the objectives of projects and gaining buy-in from key stakeholders. You can learn how to be more effective in these areas from some of the excellent books on organizational change by experts like Kotter, Robert Quinn, and Dave Ulrich.[3]

This chapter, however, focuses on the three things a top executive *cannot* delegate when trying to implement workforce and leadership changes. Earlier chapters have covered another essential step in the process. That is the leader's role in developing and clarifying objectives for talent management, given the business strategy. Once you know what results you want, even if you don't become heavily involved in the implementation process, you will greatly improve your chances of success by focusing on three critical activities described in this chapter:

- Creating urgency for results
- Clarifying role responsibilities—who does what in the implementation process?

- Requiring a holistic or integrated approach to addressing talent needs

Almost everything we have discussed in the previous chapters will be a waste of time if you don't take action in these areas. Even the most well-funded, innovative talent management solutions that are completely aligned with your business strategy will fail or seriously underdeliver if *you* don't play a critical role in these activities. You may think you don't have the time—or patience—for this. But, in your role as executive sponsor, you can have a big impact on the outcomes with relatively little time and effort. The key is focusing your attention, actions, and decisions in places that matter most.

Creating Urgency for Results

Our experience shows the biggest cause of failure in developing essential workforce and leadership capabilities is the lack of urgency needed to address these challenges. In fact, Kotter has concluded that, in general, failure to create a sense of urgency is "the number-one problem" where critical organizational change is needed but not being implemented effectively.[4] Kotter argues that the urgency needed to implement major change programs, such as talent management initiatives, is not just a matter of deciding "this is a critical issue that needs action *now* if we are to be successful." In fact, the forces undermining the sense of true urgency are insidious ones, because they are hard to recognize.

"Complacency" is particularly problematic because even leaders who feel a sense of urgency about talent-related changes may not recognize the state of employees' contentment two levels down in the organization. And, frankly, sometimes executives talk about action needed to be taken but end up communicating a sense of complacency instead.

For example, a large defense contractor is facing the loss of critical technical expertise on the major weapons systems it supports due to retirements and midcareer turnover. Leaders recognize the company's culture poses serious obstacles to retention of this essential knowledge, and they want to implement changes to improve transfer practices. The products produced by the division, however, have passed dozens of tests for its main customer, the U.S. Department of Defense, without a single failure in the last decade. This success has caused managers and employees to develop a "How bad can things be?" attitude, ignoring major potential issues in regard to critical knowledge retention. When meetings are scheduled to address the problem of knowledge transfer, the division's general manager fails to show up. He repeatedly reschedules appointments to discuss the specific programs needed to address the changing workforce. Also, responsibility for the lead knowledge sharing initiative has now been delegated to a middle manager in the IT department. Whether intended or not, the GM is clearly acting complacently about the business threats posed by the loss of critical expertise.

Organizations in government, energy, health care, and the defense sectors have experienced stable demand for so long that many employees and managers have unconsciously become immune to urgent calls for action. "Just because I get passionate about these talent issues," lamented one company president, "doesn't mean the rest of my team does. How do I get my vice presidents fired up?"

"False urgency" is the other phenomenon Kotter identifies as undermining focused, productive action on critical issues. Similar to the issue of complacency, false urgency is also common yet hard to identify because it is characterized by frenetic activity that can readily disguise real productivity. False urgency is different from "true urgency" because it is motivated by unfocused pressures that create anxiety, anger, and a fear of "losing the battle" at hand. Many organizations fall into this trap. Their leaders may recognize serious talent management threats that put their business strategy at risk (e.g., high turnover among new hires or a thin leadership pipeline). In response, they send staff members and consultants scurrying after an array of initiatives without thinking through the real priorities and risks, the specific impacts, or the resources needed. The result is "a howling wind of activity" with minimal results.[5]

To avoid the traps of complacency and false urgency, here are five key tactics for creating a *real* sense of urgency. Use these to create and sustain momentum when launching talent initiatives.

1. Connect Key Stakeholders with Reality both Outside and Inside the Organization

Those who are essential to making change happen within their organization should be exposed to the realities that make the success of their talent initiative so important. For example, Steve Carlson, CEO of Community Medical Center, wanted to increase the organization's ability to reduce medical errors, so he made sure all managers saw a short video of a patient who was the victim of a medical error and how it had affected her life. Try to find ways to bring your staff face-to-face with the external—or maybe internal—realities that make your talent initiative so crucial to the business. If you're trying to get traction on a leadership development program, maybe bring in a leading executive recruiter who can provide details on how your leadership pipeline stacks up against competitors when it comes to developing future leaders. That recruiter could also describe the realities of the changing talent marketplace. If a poor onboarding process is hurting productivity and increasing turnover, get a simple video made of recent hires recounting their experiences of joining the company (maybe include stories from those who have quit, too). Whether it is input from customers or current and past employees, the idea is to confront key players in the change process with real and valid data showing why shifts in talent management are so essential. Keep confronting them with focused—but relevant—bad news that makes the need for change ever more compelling.

2. Be Visibly Urgent in Your Daily Actions

The European general manager of a major high-tech firm reorganized his division to position the unit for a major growth spurt. He worried, however, about the lack of a succession planning process and the difficulty of holding managers accountable for talent development while the company was growing rapidly. The GM reflected, "When we restructured last year, talent was on every meeting agenda. We were continually asking, 'Do you have the right talent in place?' But talent comes and goes as a priority. You pay attention until everything is running smoothly; then you take your eyes off it until it becomes a problem again. I shouldn't have let it go off the agenda. I created the problem again." Creating urgency on talent initiatives means continually asking questions focused on talent outcomes. The trick is behaving with a daily proactive—not panicked—sense of urgency, while also maintaining a realistic perspective on the time needed for changes to take place. The downside of being unrealistically urgent is that you send subordinates into the "false urgency" mode discussed previously. Suddenly, they are busy in meetings, cranking out presentations and long trails of e-mail with virtually no results, just to please you.

Of course, how you communicate urgency in your daily actions has a lot to do with how the company is doing today. A former utility company CEO explained:

> *One of my principal responsibilities was creating urgency around issues I saw as most important. But, as we became more successful, it required greater effort to sustain that urgency. Of course, you can't have constant screaming. In situations where you're successful, but you still need to change the enterprise, your sense of urgency has to be framed in a positive way, or it's not credible. If you're achieving an 18 percent ROE and you say, "A disaster is coming," no one will believe you. So with talent management I kept asking, "Even though we're successful now, look at the age of our workforce and the lack of 19-year-old line workers. What are we going to do about this?"*

How you manifest urgency in your daily behavior will depend on your personality, the organization's culture, and even your industry. But no matter what sector you are in, it is increasingly essential for executives to communicate a sense of urgency around critical talent issues—today. One CEO of a major physicians group explained her approach, saying, "You create urgency by energizing the workforce to work *toward* particular goals, not by pressuring them constantly. That sense of urgency should be there every day. At every staff or department meeting, I ask, 'How have we thought about improving our processes?' We need to find better ways to do things."

3. Look for Opportunities in Crises

One of the best sources of urgency is when colleagues perceive something as a crisis. A key executive or technical expert leaving can energize an organization to realize it needs to invest much more effort in succession planning. Some executives will help their organizations experience a crisis vicariously, so they get the benefit of an increased sense of urgency without the actual costs. For example, a senior vice president for auditing in a major bank kept her unit focused on talent development programs by reminding colleagues that a single mistake by her team "could land the bank on the front page of the *Wall Street Journal*" in an unfavorable story. When it comes to creating urgency, never let a good potential crisis go to waste.

4. Uncover or Create Pockets of Urgency to Identify the Behaviors You Want to Promote in Your Culture

Unfortunately, you can't wait for a crisis to act on most talent issues.[6] Kotter argues that sustaining a sense of urgency is going to become the cost of staying in business, and no longer just something to drive intermittent change initiatives. That makes it all the more important to identify the leadership behaviors needed to create and sustain a true sense of urgency without burning people out. Community Medical Center CEO Steve Carlson learned an important lesson in how to create urgency when he needed an executive to drive growth in the hospital's new oncology service line. He chose an experienced director with strong leadership skills but no background in oncology. The president asked her to create a strategic plan for developing the new service line, and then he took away all her other responsibilities. "We burned the bridge to her old accountabilities," said Carlson, "and had her focus 100 percent of her time on this new role." By structuring urgency for growth into the new role, the oncology service line contributed 25 percent of the hospital's bottom line profits in the executive's first year. When the chief executive allowed another executive to juggle both operational and growth responsibilities in another service line, the urgency disappeared and growth was disappointing. Of course, behaviors that promote urgency will vary between organizations and situations. Focus on identifying the behaviors you need to promote urgency and encourage them wherever you can.

5. Don't Ignore "NoNos"

One of the most persistent killers of urgency is those individuals who relentlessly object to and resist—either overtly or covertly—any attempt at innovating around talent management. Kotter calls these urgency killers NoNos because they will do anything to kill a new idea and retain the status quo.[7] When facing talent management challenges you might hear comments such as the following:

- "We already have a performance management system. We just need to get managers to use it."
- "People have always retired, and the company survives. Why should it be any different in the future?"

- "When I joined the company I had to find my own way. Why can't we expect others to do that?"
- "If we can't find the leaders we need inside the company, we'll just go hire them."
- "We've decided not to solve that problem internally; we'll just outsource it."

Sure, these comments might come from a skeptic who has seen talent management investments wasted before and wants the firm to avoid repeating those mistakes. But a skeptic is willing to be convinced. He or she will listen to valid data and will consider well-reasoned plans to address a problem. A skeptic can be converted into an initiative champion when he or she sees the real potential of a solution.

Kotter's NoNo character is substantially different. NoNos will do anything to preserve the status quo. They are experts at undermining people who are trying to create a sense of urgency. They will regularly postpone or cancel meetings, challenge customer or workforce data as too limited, selectively use data that indicates no action is necessary, and raise anxiety about the risks of change.

Virtually every organization has NoNos, particularly those who have had relatively stable markets and workforces in years past. In our experience, the way to deal with NoNos is to shine a bright light on them. Give them measurable tasks. Hold them specifically accountable for results. Reduce their access to other people who need to follow through on the change. Let them know you are paying attention and call them out on their obstruction. Communicate consequences for failure to make the change. When you shine the bright light, one of two things will happen: they will step up and be successful, or they will find another job. Either way, they are no longer NoNos.

Creating and sustaining a sense of urgency is your biggest challenge when it comes to implementing solutions related to talent management. Talent initiatives often address critical long-term issues that don't have an immediate impact on performance. In the meantime, there will be plenty of operational issues and "brush fires" to distract you and your staff. Of course, staying focused on what is truly important for the long-term health of the firm will at times require great perseverance and courage.

Who Does What in Talent Initiatives? Clarifying Role Responsibilities

When you find yourself in the role of "executive sponsor" for talent initiatives, how do you ensure you're doing your part, given how little time you likely have to spend on talent issues? This section will show you how to play an effective sponsorship role, even when your time is limited. But first, here's what can happen when executive sponsors don't do their jobs at different stages of the talent management process.

A company that operates one of the largest natural gas pipelines in the United States was facing serious challenges to sustaining profitable operations. A major concern was the projected loss of 50 percent of its veteran workforce within the next decade. More specifically, within five years almost a quarter of the workforce would be 60 or older. This group performed a high percentage of the most critical tasks in the business and held much of the company's institutional knowledge. Given the seriousness of the threat, the vice president of operations sponsored a task force including 34 employees to diagnose the problem and propose solutions. He provided only general instructions, asking that the group make recommendations about dealing with the aging workforce, retaining a new generation of employees, and bridging potential knowledge gaps.

The task force worked in multiple daylong planning sessions for six months without further interaction with its sponsor. Even though it understood the strategic implications of the aging workforce, the executive sponsor's vague request gave no clear direction to the group and included no follow-up. Not surprisingly, the task force produced only a vaguely worded report with general findings that the sponsor felt was unhelpful. As a result, no specific solutions were pursued. This meant that 34 of this firm's best, busiest people had just wasted their time for six months—*at the vice president's request*. Even worse, no progress had been made in addressing critical workforce threats.

In another case, a VP of engineering in the Canadian-based division of a global software company was asked to sponsor a management development program. The unit had been plagued by ineffective management of its software developers and high turnover among supervisors, which threatened the firm's growth plans. The division's HR department had engaged a consulting firm to design a new leadership development program. When asked to approve the initiative, the VP said simply, "That sounds great. We need that." In the next few months, the program was developed with substantial input from successful frontline and mid-tier leaders across the division. Morale rose in anticipation of its rollout. Then, at the last minute, the European-based headquarters got word of the project and killed it. Apparently, their policies required that the Canadian division use existing corporate resources for management training rather than develop their own. The engineering VP's failure to clarify responsibilities for training by asking his HR team the right questions wasted three months of effort designing the new management development program, further demoralized the staff, and delayed any benefits that would be created by improving supervisory skills.

How to Be an Effective Sponsor

Of course, leaders can oversee successful talent initiatives in several ways. At one end of the spectrum a top manager can be very "high touch," setting goals, recruiting support, monitoring the project plan, sitting in on every meeting, ensuring every dollar is well spent, and pouring the celebratory bubbly when the whole thing is over. At the other end of the spectrum, a sponsor might be merely a figurehead who gives a brief kickoff speech and then jets away, expecting a quick note about the results in a future status report.

When it comes to effective sponsorship, the critical success factor is to be clear about expectations up front both for yourself and for those who are expecting your help. As the executive sponsor, you have an obligation to ensure the initiative is likely to be successful. One way to do this is by building a coalition of people who will play key roles in making the change happen. The more complex the organization and the initiative, the more essential coalition-building becomes.[8] Part of this coalition-building step is to identify and clarify who will play central roles in the implementation process. For example, if the team proposing the initiative cannot provide an owner/driver for the key components required to make the project successful, then you either need to provide that support or consider withholding sponsorship.

Whenever you find yourself as the likely sponsor for a talent management program, be sure to clarify who is going to play specific roles in the initiative. If not you, then who will do it? Here is a checklist you can use in less than an hour to clarify roles. This will greatly increase the chances your project will succeed.

The Responsibility Assignment Matrix (or RASCI Model), is a proven tool for clarifying roles in sponsorship situations.[9] For each task in the left-hand column of Table 9.1 on pages 219–21, identify who is going to be:

R **Responsible.** The person who is owner/project manager of a particular task.
A **Accountable.** The person to whom "R" is accountable who is the authority that approves/signs off on budget and work before it is undertaken.
S **Supportive.** A person who is doing "hands-on" work for the project implementation.
C **Consulted.** A person who provides essential information and/or expertise necessary to complete the project.
I **Informed.** A person who just needs to be notified of results but need not be consulted during implementation.

In reviewing the Responsibility Assignment Matrix, you have two jobs: to spell out your own role, and to clarify your expectations of the project owner. Often, many of these tasks could be done by multiple people, but if you don't clarify these responsibilities up front you're much more likely to have work that goes undone or may experience overlapping efforts. Table 9.1 includes some suggestions for minimum sponsor activities to guide you. We've left the "project owner" column blank because often the project owner's role will be tailored to fill in where you (the sponsor) leave off. Go through each step carefully with the project owner to avoid some of the most common mistakes. For example, if the VP of operations at the gas pipeline company mentioned earlier had worked through this list with the head of the task force, he would have realized that *no one* saw himself or herself as the owner of critical first steps, such as writing clear goals and success metrics and clarifying stakeholders. In fact, what he would have noticed is that the only thing the task force saw as its role was *one line* in the matrix—to consider existing solutions from within the company or within the industry. In effect, the task force spent months looking at solutions without ever really understanding the problem.

No matter how little time you have to devote to talent management, the key as an executive sponsor is to clarify expectations, remove ambiguity, and improve the likelihood that the effort will be successful. When implementing new initiatives, take an hour to work through Table 9.1 with the project owner to clarify some of the most important tasks. If, as you review this list, you find yourself unable to do more than participate as "I," informed, the project is very likely to fail—even with the most competent project owner on board. Your options at that point are to reset your own priorities, recruit another sponsor (using Table 9.1 to ensure that sponsor is able to do the job), or pull the plug on the project. All of these options are far better than allowing your talent management team to pursue a project that is likely to fail.

TABLE 9.1   Essential Roles for Talent Management Activities

Task	Sponsor's Role	Project Owner's Role	Comments
Define/agree on a business reason for the talent management project, may include relating the project to strategic workforce plan	Could be "R," "A," or "S"— minimally "C"; red flag if only an "I"		This is the most important first step for an executive sponsor.
Clarify who will participate in the project and why	Probably "C" or "I"		Include those who will directly benefit from the project.
Lead meetings, manage deliverables, provide status	Often an "I"		Discuss the stages where you might take a higher-profile role.
Identify stakeholders (internal customers or potential resisters, in addition to the sponsor)	Should be "R" or "S"— minimally "C"; red flag if only an "I"		Recruiting stakeholders and identifying potential roadblocks is a critical role for a sponsor.
Set goals and success metrics for the project	Minimally a "C"; red flag if only an "I"		Sponsor ensures goals have a clear connection to business problem.
Consider existing solutions from within the company or within the industry	Probably "C" or "I"		

(continued)

TABLE 9.1   Essential Roles for Talent Management Activities *(continued)*

Task	Sponsor's Role	Project Owner's Role	Comments
Gather any relevant history/lessons learned on previous attempts to solve this problem	Probably "C" or "I"		
Secure funding for the project	Should be "R" or "S"		A core function for a sponsor
Choose a solution for the talent management problem	Probably "C" or "I"		
Write operational plans to implement the project	Probably "C" or "I"		
Review plans and provide feedback	Minimally "S"		Even the busiest sponsor should expect to do this.
Recruit participants (i.e., those who directly benefit)	Probably "C" or "I"		Projects often fail when the "right" people do not attend.
Recruit talent (authors, presenters, mentors, and so on)	Could be "S," "C," or "I"		
Appear personally as a participant or speaker at an event	If appearing, would be "S"		

Task	Sponsor's Role	Project Owner's Role	Comments
Persuade/gain buy-in from other leaders	Should be "R" or "S"—minimally a "C"; red flag if only an "I"		Using political capital is a core function of a sponsor.
Conduct a risk analysis (fiscal, organizational, political) to assess barriers to success	Minimally "C"; red flag if only an "I"		
Review and communicate results to stakeholders	Could be "S," "C," or "I"		

Note that this is a detailed list of activities because part of your role as sponsor is to ensure that the project ownership is clear, even when you are not personally involved.

Of course, these are not all the tasks where an executive sponsor should play a role in a talent management initiative. Table 9.1 just shows some of the most essential ones and illustrates the explicit choices that should be made about the top manager's actual level of involvement to ensure the project's success. Whenever key activities are identified in the implementation process, brief but explicit discussions should be held to clarify what roles you and others are going to play in completing the task.

How to Drive a More Holistic, Integrated Approach to Talent Management

When the new chief executive took over at a major power generating station, he found an uncoordinated cadre of consultants working on different projects that affected workforce development. Faced with a huge group of highly skilled engineers and operators about to retire, the executive had to establish and implement a more focused and integrated talent development agenda if the plant was to meet its performance objectives.

In another case, the vice president for clinical trials in a fast-growing medical devices company needed to expand his staff to support the rollout of a promising new product in the next year. The success of this new product introduction, projected to generate more than $500 million in revenues, would depend on the ability of the firm's highly skilled clinical specialists to help doctors use the product safely and effectively. With only a dozen clinical specialists currently on staff for the small clinical trial, the VP was worried about the company's ability to add the hundreds of specialists needed to launch the product. In conversations with the HR department, he knew there was still only a brief job description available and no onboarding program in place for the new employees.

The sophistication of talent management infrastructures varies greatly from organization to organization. A growing number of firms like Aetna, IBM, and McDonald's have advanced talent management processes that allow them to anticipate workforce changes and respond quickly to shifts in market demand. But many other organizations—large and small—are still struggling to build out the most basic talent processes. Therefore, the need for a more holistic approach and greater integration will have different meanings depending on a company's situation.

Terminology: Holistic Thinking Versus Integration and Coordination

When it comes to talent management, thinking holistically encompasses more than just integration or coordination, although these words are often used interchangeably. The terms actually imply different objectives or perspectives, so it is important to be clear what you mean. Sometimes a leader's objective is to *integrate* different elements, activities, or processes that make up the overall talent management life cycle to form a larger subsystem or process. For example, this may mean combining a diverse set of training programs into one seamless training system to eliminate redundancies and improve synergies from the different offerings. At other times, executives need to improve the *coordination* between different parts of a talent management system. In that case, a leader might be trying to tighten the relationship and linkages between steps in the employee life cycle, such as improving coordination between recruiting and onboarding practices. Whether the goal is improved integration or coordination, what is common in both cases is an attempt to think more holistically or systemically about talent management. This is more than a semantic argument. Lots of time and resources can be wasted when leaders aren't clear about their objectives.

Although the need for "integrated talent management" has been recognized in many HR departments, there are actually three different ways leaders can encourage a more integrated approach to talent management and add value in this area.

1. Examine Talent Programs from the User's Perspective and Focus on Handoffs

Examine existing and proposed talent programs from the user's perspective and focus particularly on the handoffs between different stages in the process. For example, the vice president at the medical devices company should be asking the head of HR these questions: Can you tell me about the experiences of newly hired clinical specialists from the time they're recruited until they have been on the job for four months? What happens when they first arrive at the company? What happens after they finish HR's new hire orientation? How do they transition to the team or unit they were hired into? Once with their new team, how do they get integrated into formal training programs?

As an executive, what you're listening for is the quality of the transitions between steps in the talent management process. Is the handoff between recruiting and onboarding smooth? Will the new employee be clearly and efficiently directed into the formal training needed to become fully productive? (See sidebar, "Discovering the Employee's View of Your Talent Processes.") These handoffs in the employee life cycle are often remarkably uncoordinated. For example, in one utility company the HR department was unable to provide a report to the engineering division on who had accepted job offers and when they would start work.

If the answers to your questions about transitions in the employee life cycle are unsatisfactory, the first consideration is how critical the affected roles are. If poor handoffs were slowing down the onboarding of a few customer service reps, for example, you might not be too concerned. But for the medical products VP who needs to train hundreds of new clinical specialists to support a major new product launch, having a highly coordinated talent management process will be critical for business growth. The obvious question is, How can your staff smooth out those transitions or connections between stages in the talent life cycle?

Discovering the Employee's View of Your Talent Processes

Here are some questions to ask from the employee's or potential employee's perspective to better understand what happens at each stage in the employee life cycle (recruiting, onboarding, development, retention). When asking these questions, listen for the "handoff" from one stage to the next and for any places where the ball (in this case the employee) is dropped and left to his or her own devices. These questions do not require a formal "program." Just make sure there are logical answers that show continuity, a sense of integration where practical, and a holistic perspective.

As a potential employee or new hire:

- How do I find out about these open positions?
- What happens to my résumé or phone call when I ask about an open position?
- Who is my first point of contact when I show up for an interview? Who participates in the interview? If people interviewing me can't answer questions about the organization's strategy (outlined in Chapter 3), how will that affect how I am treated?

(continued)

- Once I'm offered a job, what interactions do I have with the company up until the beginning of my first day? Who is responsible for those interactions, and what steps do they take before I arrive to set a new employee up for success?
- How am I handed off from recruiting/staffing to onboarding and ultimately to the team where I will be working?
- Once I'm hired, what does my first day look like? Assuming I spend some time on HR paperwork right away, what happens next?
- What has my new team done to prepare for my arrival? Describe my first day on the job with my hiring team.
- At the end of my first week on the job, what questions should I be able to answer to show that I'm on the right track? For example, Whom have I met? Is my workstation set up? Do I have a plan for my skill development? Do I have a mentor?
- At the end of my first quarter on the job, what questions should I be able to answer to show that I'm on the right track? For example, Whom have I met? What skills have I developed? What goals have I set and achieved? What are my plans for the coming quarter? Do I understand how my work fits into the big picture?
- How will I be asked about my experiences during these first months on the job to ensure I feel like I'm learning and contributing to a high degree and that I feel confident in my future with the company?
- At the end of my first year or my first performance review cycle, can I speak to those same questions, plus can I describe the feedback I've received and how that is influencing my progress and direction?

- If I lead people, what additional experiences will I have? For example, management training?
- If I have performance problems, what experiences will I have?
- After 18 months on the job, what information will the organization know about the value I bring to the company and my potential for the future?
- How are my skills developed over the course of my tenure with the company? What is expected of me in driving this? What support do I get from the organization?

2. Stop, Take Inventory, and Clarify Priorities and Sequencing of Initiatives

A lot of organizations today have many talent management initiatives in various stages of design and use. One aerospace company found it had dozens of mentoring programs in use. Executives, like the new head of the power generating station, can feel overwhelmed at times when trying to make sense of the organization's current and future talent management processes. The first step if things seem out of control is to take an inventory as described in Chapter 5. You may have a mish-mash of talent programs and processes whose connections are unclear. Or there may seem to be too many pilots and programs under development. Or maybe there are too many well-intentioned consultants running around the organization working on disconnected talent-related projects.

No matter what the source of confusion is, the underlying issue is competing priorities, which means you probably have some great people working very hard on the wrong things. Doing an inventory of talent initiatives is the first step to realigning those efforts with strategic business needs. It allows you to develop and communicate a clear message about priorities. For example, maybe employees are being asked to participate in both a knowledge retention program and a new onboarding pilot to accelerate new hire productivity. Both projects sound important, but where should managers allocate their limited resources? Maybe the knowledge retention effort has to take priority for the next quarter because 20 people with know-how critical to the business are about to retire. Management can focus on onboarding after that. When it comes to prioritizing and coordinating talent initiatives, sequencing can be key.

3. Break Down Barriers Between Silos to Increase Organizational Agility

Insurance giant Aetna went through a major setback a few years ago when it acquired a number of firms whose subsequent performance was poor. In turning Aetna around, the CEO's main priority was to create talent management processes that identified and developed the workforce skills needed to support the company's evolving business portfolio. Thus, over five years, the chief executive oversaw the implementation of an integrated approach to talent management that included skills assessment, skills development, and performance management processes that were ultimately built into the overall business planning process. Thus, if Aetna were to reorganize today, top management can quickly find the best candidates to fill new positions.[10]

Some firms, like Aetna, need leaders who can push a change agenda that focuses on creating an integrated talent management and business planning process. But relatively few organizations have reached this stage. The more common scenario will reflect a U.K. study of large companies that found only 1 of 16 firms reporting any coordination between its recruiting, management development, and talent management functions. Most organizations still treat these as separate functions with limited interaction.[11]

Thus, even when individual talent functions are well established, top management should be asking hard questions about why these silos are not better coordinated or integrated. It may be that leadership has to create the structure to make this change happen. Top management in one major high-tech firm did this by creating a cross-functional task force with the mandate to build an integrated workplace strategy supporting the firm's business goals and culture. Leaders made it clear they were holding functional heads in HR and IT accountable for the same goals—effectively improving employee productivity and engagement. The structure and mandate of the cross-functional task force meant each group was heavily invested in developing a more integrated solution.

In other organizations, the integration challenge won't be restructuring talent functions. That may come later. For now, the issue that needs leadership attention may be integrating critical data that can be used by management to make better talent-related decisions. Questions that drive integration are often likely to be asked around the implementation and use of IT systems supporting talent management:

- Will this IT investment produce data from different talent management activities that improves executive decision making? For example, will data from succession planning processes trigger leadership development programs to allow more effective decisions about top management participation in these sessions?

- Are we trying to integrate talent management technology with old behaviors? Or are we also investing in creating new behaviors to maximize the capabilities of the new system? For example, automating the performance review process does no good if, historically, managers have not used data from these reviews in their decision making.

How Will You Drive Change?

When it comes to improving talent management, your focus may be on fixing specific problems, such as retaining more high potentials, or on using talent initiatives to help transform the organization's culture. Regardless of your objectives, it is a huge mistake to ignore the dynamics of change management when trying to improve workforce and leadership capabilities. If talent is truly critical to your firm's profitability, then you can't afford to increase your chances of failure by ignoring your role in the implementation process. In the end, leaders get the greatest payoff by focusing on the three activities described here: creating and sustaining urgency for the changes needed, clarifying roles and responsibilities for the initiative, and driving integration wherever possible.

In the new economy, talent management challenges are continually evolving. New issues are emerging every year. Chapter 10 focuses on the latest challenges and opportunities we found in our most recent research and concludes with specific action steps to get started.

For Talent Management and HR Business Partners

Producing Results: Supporting and Guiding Executive Sponsors

For talent management initiatives, buy-in and support from senior leaders is one of the most important determinants of success. That's why it is imperative for these leaders to show the urgency they feel around talent management issues.

As a talent management leader, you can help top managers appropriately support talent management by developing your own ideas of how executives could communicate urgency. For example, if you were to imagine the two or three things top executives in your organization could be doing to create urgency around a particular problem, what would they be? What conversations should the executives have? What arms should be twisted? What resources would need to be budgeted? What data should be shared? What priorities would be set?

Once you have that picture, you can think about obstacles to business leaders' participation and work to remove those obstacles. Are competing priorities the obstacle? Lack of information? Your own failure to communicate urgency to the business line executive? What is getting in the way of them helping to communicate urgency, and what can you do about it?

With these insights, you can make your own action plan for creating urgency:

- Gather the data needed to connect key stakeholders to reality. This could include preparing a needs and/or risk

(continued)

analysis, distributing books and articles, or benchmark-
ing against companies in your industry or region.
- Show urgency yourself. Invite executives to meetings,
give them language to describe urgency, insist that there
not be too many "number one" priorities.
- Use a crisis to demonstrate the importance of the change
you seek.
- Learn from colleagues. When you see an executive who
is appropriately creating urgency, apply that person's
techniques to your own situation.

As a talent management leader, you may not have the direct
authority to create urgency. But you can use your vision of
what should happen to build urgency, as described previously. Similarly, when working with an executive sponsor,
you can use your own vision for the sponsor's activities as
a basis to clarify roles, think about potential concerns, and
encourage the sponsor to strongly support talent management
activities.

Another essential executive function is assuring that all talent management activities work together. Talent management
leaders can support this role by taking a look at the employee
life cycle all the way from before a potential candidate is
interviewed through to the employee's five-year anniversary,
paying particular attention to what happens as new employees
are handed off from one stage to the next. Are these transitions from recruiting to onboarding, or from onboarding to the
hiring team smooth, and if not, what can you do to improve
them? This involves looking at the whole employee experience,

not just individual talent management activities. And, since talent management is often shared between HR and many other players, it often means looking across departments and between groups that don't always talk to each other. You can be the liaison who ensures that each employee moves quickly and efficiently through the employee life cycle.

10

Managing Talent in
the New Economy

Six Lessons from the Leading Edge

Talent management has a long way to go in many organizations. In researching this book, we interviewed more than 70 senior executives and leading talent experts to better understand what made senior managers more or less effective in this increasingly important area. Executives' comments show that the state of talent management in major corporations and large businesses needs significant improvement. They indicate that talent management isn't as far along as it ought to be, given its obvious importance.

Some themes recurred time and time again. In this concluding chapter, we leave you with six lessons based on insights from our interviews. Acting on these principles will make you a more effective leader when it comes to managing talent:

- Make it clear who "owns" talent management in your organization. (Hint: It's not HR.)
- Know the talent management IQ of your executive team.

- Stop the hoarding of high potentials.
- Develop tomorrow's leadership skills today.
- Manage performance as if talent really matters.
- Make sure your board of directors is contributing to top-level talent conversations.

1. Make It Clear Who "Owns" Talent Management in Your Organization

Does the finance department own an organization's financial assets? No. But in many firms there's an implicit assumption that the HR department controls talent management, and that's the kiss of death. When talent management is seen as an HR function, business leaders abdicate responsibility. Talent management becomes a tangential function—overhead, if you will. One senior talent executive in financial services proposed that, in order to protect its political turf, HR was attempting to maintain authority over the talent management process. Ironically, this approach reduces talent management's effectiveness, with the consequent loss of prestige and clout: "HR hasn't taught the business side how to do this because we need a job," confessed the executive. "But trying to do this for the business doesn't work."

"The question is, What does 'owning the people agenda' mean?" asked a high-tech talent executive. Those we interviewed insist controlling the agenda starts with a talent management mind-set. Leaders and managers throughout the organization have to feel a responsibility for developing people, instead of just producing results. Making this responsibility a widespread feeling among managers is definitely a work in progress, even for the best companies.

Talent management must serve a real business need. That's the consensus in organizations that have had early successes in this area. It is not just "something HR does." For example, a few years ago Cisco's CEO John Chambers was hesitant to make talent management part of his own agenda. What he was most concerned about was creating the structures and culture needed to drive collaboration throughout the organization. When Chambers initially resisted the talent focus, Annmarie Neal, his savvy chief talent executive, began addressing the problem of helping the CEO shift the organization from a traditional command-and-control to a collaborative leadership culture. Working with colleagues, Neal started the Center for Collaborative Leadership at Cisco, which became a centerpiece of the firm's succession planning and leadership development efforts.[1] "We used talent management to address what kept the CEO up at night," explained Neal. "It was about building collaboration capabilities, which also supported what the sales force was selling." Tying talent objectives to top management's business goals built ownership where it needed to be. Over time, Cisco's CEO became an avid proponent of talent management, and it is now viewed as a central responsibility of managers.

Here's one way to make it clear who "owns" talent management. "Create a committee of senior leaders chaired by the chief executive that also includes the head of HR," says Jo Moore, SVP of Organizational Development for Caliper Consulting. The discussion starts in a strategic frame, looking at the big picture questions discussed in Chapter 3: Where is the business going? What is the strategy for growth? What's changing in the marketplace? Then the logical link is, What kinds of talent are needed, given the strategy? How are we building a pipeline of people who can step into different roles? The first step to establishing ownership of the talent management agenda is getting leaders in the habit of proactively asking these questions. That's because, ultimately, HR can't be the face of talent management.

2. Know the Talent Management IQ of Your Executive Team

When trying to build a talent mind-set among your leadership team, it's essential to know whom and what you're working with. Not all executives, of course, believe that developing people is an essential part of their job. One major consumer products company puts its leaders in categories when it comes to managing talent:

- *Innovators* are executives who will continually come up with new requirements, proposals, or insights that improve the firm's talent practices and processes. For example, this firm's CEO has repeatedly come up with ideas for making senior talent review meetings more productive.
- *Champions* are leaders who proactively recognize that developing talent is an essential part of their roles to maximize performance of the business, so they will enthusiastically support new initiatives brought to them by the talent management staff.
- *Conformers* are top managers who will at least comply with routine processes and practices for developing people. For example, when do these performance reviews need to be done? These executives are willing to invest

the time if they are guided through structured talent management activities.

- *Laggards* are leaders so caught up in the day-to-day operations that they struggle to understand how to plan for talent development or how to use the reward system to motivate employees. They can't think holistically about the employee life cycle, and they don't understand how they might leverage the workforce to be an asset to their business.

What category are you in? How would you rate the members of your team? The head of talent management in one leading high-tech firm estimates about 35 percent of his executives are innovators or champions. About 40 percent comply with existing talent management processes, and 25 percent "will never get it."

When hiring or promoting new leaders, ask whether they are innovators or champions when it comes to talent management. Can you really afford to promote laggards into leadership roles where talent development is essential to organizational performance? When you promote people to executive positions today it is critical to be conscious about their aptitudes for managing talent. If your leadership pipeline proves to be short on these capabilities, then you need to invest in this area.

3. Stop the Hoarding of High Potentials

There has been a lot written about the importance of identifying your most critical talent management needs and concentrating the firm's investments in those areas.[2] We addressed the importance of priority setting in Chapters 3 and 4. But, like all good plans, maximizing the use of talent management resources is much harder than it sounds.

One of the most common challenges for CEOs and general managers is getting their leadership teams to take on an organization-wide or systemic view of managing talent. Hoarding high potentials is an ongoing problem, since functional and business unit leaders can be very protective of their own top talent. This is a particular problem when executives feel they have no adequate replacement for a star performer they might lose.

Smart leaders create systems to develop cultural norms that treat high-potential talent as an organization-wide resource. For example, a United Kingdom–based global consumer products firm set up a series of talent review meetings to make sure employees with the greatest potential get visibility outside their regions. At the global functional review, regional marketing managers discuss their high potentials with the global director so promising talent becomes more widely recognized. Executives at New York Life are now measured on the number of high potentials they export to other parts of the company. In addition, top management tracks the percentage of people an executive includes from outside his or her unit in the current succession planning chart. This forces unit leaders to become familiar with talent elsewhere in the firm.

Good talent management means valuing high potentials as an organizational asset; it also means focusing talent resources on critical roles in the business. This isn't always as easy as it sounds. Top management in a global consumer products company voiced support for a differentiated workforce strategy. But when employee surveys showed the firm scoring low on career development opportunities, leaders suddenly felt pressure to invest resources in talent development for the general workforce. Senior executives may find themselves continually confronting trade-offs. Do you want managers to focus primarily on developing and retaining high potentials in key roles? Or, will managers be rewarded more for sustaining high levels of employee engagement and lower overall turnover? In some cases, leaders are very concerned about alienating those employees not designated as high potentials. But, as one top talent coach points out, the essential question is, "Would you rather retain top talent or minimize upset?"[3] The balancing act is always getting the greatest return on your talent management investment to drive the business.

4. Develop Tomorrow's Leadership Skills Today

It's always difficult to see over the horizon, but smart executives know that some of the leadership skills needed in the future will be considerably different than what's needed today. Some of the capabilities your organization needs will be driven by its growth and the natural evolution of the business. Other capabilities will be necessary because of the changing competitive environment, increased globalization, and the proliferation of Web 2.0 and communication technologies. The question top management must continually be asking is, Are we identifying and developing the essential leadership capabilities needed for the future?[4] "It's one thing to have enough people in the talent pipeline," said a utility company executive. "It is quite another to make sure the pipeline is producing leaders with the values and styles you will need in the future."

The COO of a major health-care system, for example, is worried about developing leaders who think systemically enough to oversee an integrated health-care delivery system. "We get leaders who are good performers in a specific domain, like critical care or oncology, but we need a better process to teach them how to lead five hospitals and 70 clinics as an integrated organization." While these leadership skills have existed in the past, they take time to develop, and the demand for them is growing as organizations become increasingly integrated, networked, and global. Thus, more and more companies will be looking for leaders who can think at a systems level.

Communication has always been a core leadership capability, but executives will find it increasingly necessary to master the use of Web 2.0 technologies to interact with their employees, customers, suppliers, and investors. Leaders in one oldline diversified industrial firm recognize that their younger employees expect access to a variety of communication channels. This company has started an employee portal where the CEO posts articles and blogs about why he finds them important. Other executives are using video to communicate details and background on recent performance results. These evolving communication channels will require the time and attention of leaders who want to be effective in the future.

Other leadership competencies require special attention today so they will be available in the years ahead. For example, top managers at one of the world's most innovative consumer products firms recognize that future leaders must have the cultural sensitivity needed to develop productive relationships quickly with potential partners, suppliers, and customers throughout the world. A top R&D executive in the United Kingdom, for example, might be dealing with scientists in China today, engineers in Germany tomorrow, and project managers in Brazil next week. "Cultural sensitivity is key for organizations that want to grow," argues Chris Thoen, P&G's director of global business development, external innovation, and knowledge management. One of the most important things top managers can do today is identify the leadership skills essential to the *future* of the business. Then make sure you are surrounding yourself with the talent needed to develop and deliver those capabilities as quickly as possible.

5. Manage Performance as if Talent Really Matters

One of the most consistent themes in our research is the widespread frustration among executives that their organizations are hurt by poor performance management. "I am continually amazed that so many high-achieving executives tolerate mediocrity. Leaders tend not to raise the performance bar for others," says John Boyle, a consulting partner with the Clarion Group, who has worked extensively with executive teams. One quick way to see if you are part of this problem is to answer these three questions honestly:

- What's your success rate in hiring your direct reports?
- Think of your worst hire. How long did it take you to recognize the mistake?
- How long was it before you dealt with this mistake?

Professor Les Charm, an expert in small company governance at Babson College, gets a kick out of asking these questions of CEOs, who consistently report it takes them at least nine months to deal with bad hires. If top managers have trouble addressing performance issues, then it is no surprise that the failure to hold executives accountable for performance problems is a widespread organizational issue. "There is a financial risk in not managing poor performance, but we just don't hold people accountable for this," said one exasperated high-tech leader. "We shouldn't promote people who don't manage talent well."

A leader in another global high-tech firm recalled introducing a succession planning process to top management, initially resulting in a great deal of eye rolling from managers. "Nobody took it seriously until the next year," he said. "When I added a column showing that we had only hired 200 managers, when we needed 500—that got people's attention. Then the CEO started holding people accountable and everything changed." The point is to look at your own behavior around performance management first, and estimate the time you are spending on C-players, instead of replacing them. Then collect other data that show the business costs of failing to hold your team accountable for poor performance in managing talent.[5] Those are the first steps to reversing the negative effects of poor performance management.

6. Make Sure Your Board of Directors Is Contributing to Top-Level Talent Conversations

Some boards get it, but many clearly don't. If talent is an increasingly central asset of many organizations, then their boards of directors must be more proactive in monitoring the chief executive's agenda in this area. At Procter & Gamble, directors devote an entire meeting every year to reviewing succession plans for the top 35 jobs in the company. The goal is to review three possible candidates for each position.[6] McDonald's is another company where the board takes succession planning and talent very seriously. This global food service retailer lost three CEOs in two years, when two chief executives suffered fatal health problems. The McDonald's board expects its CEO to have detailed plans in place for rapid succession should anything happen to a top executive. The tragic events of recent years have strongly reinforced this need.

These companies are exceptions, according to John Gillespie and David Zweig, experts on the performance of corporate boards.[7] "Talent management and succession policy are key areas for boards to monitor," says Zweig. "But they usually get ignored because succession becomes analogous to dealing with death." Gillespie points out, "Boards overwhelmingly deal with the past, but talent management is an issue focused on the future. So, even though talent risks are critical issues for boards, they get little or no attention. That's ironic because, if you're a steward of the long-term viability of the business, talent is the only real asset in many organizations today."

Of course, boards in some firms have begun playing an important role in the talent management discussion. At New York Life, CEO Ted Mathas updates his board regularly on succession management plans for the top 70 jobs and the challenges involved in filling them. For an East Coast utility, the CEO reports annually on the development plans she has in place for the executives who might succeed her. When she was promoted to chief executive, the board also collaborated with her to identify areas, such as regulatory issues, where she needed additional knowledge.

The contribution of boards in reviewing talent management strategies will depend on the organization's needs, top management's expectations, and the expertise individual directors bring to talent issues. Savvy executives should expect boards to hold them more accountable in this area in the future, but that can only happen if organizations choose directors with the experience and wisdom to guide leaders on critical talent issues.

Improving Your Chances of Success

This book has focused heavily on executive tasks such as aligning talent needs with strategy, prioritizing talent risks, and evaluating current and potential solutions. Ultimately, to improve results in managing talent, our research shows effective leaders focus on changing behaviors—their own and that of their executive team, for starters. First of all, you need to demonstrate that recruiting, developing, and retaining talent is the responsibility of line management—not HR. One way to do that is to engage managers to look at talent at a very personal level. What is it going to do for their organizations? You need to help them make the connection between the quality of their talent and the desired results. Dialogue is the key to developing a talent mind-set in your line executives, and it can take time and many conversations to do so. "It's not about *telling* people in a PowerPoint presentation," said a senior executive in a global consumer products company. "It's about going through a process. You don't get buy-in from managers unless you make them think and listen to what they say."

Another behavioral change you want is to maximize the sharing of talent across the organization. Do you know where your most promising high potentials are working in your firm today? Is there a chance they are still being hidden by divisional or functional leaders? A top executive for one global beverage company said, "When we anticipate growth in certain markets today, the top team will ask, 'Who can go into those markets? Who can fill that role to drive growth?' We play chess, thinking three or four moves out to make sure we're putting the best people against real opportunities. Instead, we used to say, 'Oh God, we've got a vacancy in Turkey or China. Who's going to fill it?'"

To improve talent sharing, you will have to examine how you are rewarding or penalizing good talent managers today. Are there conflicting norms in the culture? If you are still primarily rewarding leaders for short-term execution, then why shouldn't they hoard talent? As the saying goes, "Are you rewarding for A, but still hoping for B?"[8] Effective top managers make sure they are continuously demonstrating through performance reviews and promotions that managing talent effectively is a core value in the organization. Here's how a global consumer products firm with operations in 180 countries now reinforces the accountability of its managers for leadership development. One senior executive explained:

> When top managers visit different units, they always ask, "Show us your leadership talent pipeline." In the past, maybe the local HR department would present. But today business leaders must demonstrate what they're doing to keep their talent pipeline healthy. These guys know they will be grilled on who their best people are. And top executives want to meet the key talent in different countries. Managers either

take pride in who they are developing or are ashamed. It's your ticket to being promoted, or it's a black mark against you, if you're not developing talent.

Finally, effective executives continually promote the development of new capabilities in their teams. They focus on the future and what new leadership competencies the organization needs to get there. The CEO of a financial services company realized his firm had to reinvent itself to stay profitable in a rapidly changing market. In reorganizing his executive team, this chief executive had to decide who had the leadership capabilities that would be essential to drive the company in a new direction. He needed executives who could think more strategically and collaborate across boundaries to shape the agenda of a more diversified company. In choosing his new team, the CEO was forced to leave some more senior executives behind, opting instead for several younger leaders who had demonstrated the technical expertise and collaborative capabilities that could shape the new organization. Relentlessly looking to the future and identifying what new skills are needed to get there, and beyond, will be a hallmark of effective leadership in the years ahead.

What's Your Next Step?

Where and how you focus on managing talent will, of course, depend on your role in the organization, your industry, the size of your company, and the state of your existing talent management infrastructure. You may be the CEO of a major multinational corporation, the general manager in a small but fast-growing firm, or a director in a nonprofit or government agency. Regardless of your position, as an executive, your ability to lead and focus the efforts of your staff on critical talent management initiatives will have a tremendous impact on both your personal success and the success of your organization.

Most leaders are not prepared for the responsibilities of overseeing efforts to develop changing workforce and leadership capabilities, and many, frankly, are not particularly interested in these tasks. The CEO of one of the world's largest retailers would much rather talk about his stores and the financial aspects of his highly profitable business. But he realizes his most essential task is creating a robust leadership pipeline. Thus, he has been careful to set aside his strong interest in operations. He continues instead to invest his time and resources in making talent management a strategic priority for the company. Regardless of your personal interest in managing talent, our goal has been to give you the essentials you need to have an immediate impact on your organization's workforce and leadership capabilities.

What's Your "Commander's Intent"?

As a leader, you face countless requests for your time and support. Ultimately, your success depends on your ability to relentlessly focus your organization on the few priorities that are critical to success. In the U.S. Army they call this "Commander's Intent."[9] If your intent, as a leader, is to manage talent effectively, and to align the behaviors and decisions of your staff in this direction, then you now have the tools needed to take effective action. Depending on your situation, there are seven specific things you should do to be effective in talent management:

1. **Decide what role you are going to play.** As we indicated in Chapters 1 and 2, this depends on your immediate situation and your most critical talent needs. Do you already have a relatively sophisticated talent management infrastructure run by HR? Are you faced with a critical short-term problem, such as experts retiring, that must be addressed? Or are you starting a talent effort from scratch? Each of these scenarios will require a different approach. You can use the Responsibility Assignment Matrix in Chapter 9 to get started.

2. **Develop a clear, shared understanding of specifically what people in your organization mean by "talent management."** You may use other concepts, such as "strategic workforce development" or "human capital management." But don't invest time and resources in these things until you are sure everyone understands what they mean. Insist that whatever terms are used in your culture are clearly defined. That's the essential first step in communicating the outcomes you expect.

3. **Make sure your staff can articulate the strategic big picture.** This is the most effective way to ensure that talent initiatives are directly tied to your business strategy. Answering the big picture questions in Chapter 3 will also support objectives for increasing employee engagement.

4. **Critically evaluate the processes and tools you are currently using to identify and prioritize talent-related risks.** Beware of overconfidence when it comes to qualitative risk analysis methodologies. At the same time, make sure your staff is doing enough to identify *specific* knowledge at risk with a tool like the Knowledge Silo Matrix described in Chapter 4.

5. **Evaluate the alignment of your current culture with the talent management initiatives you are pursuing.** Use Table 5.2 in Chapter 5 to surface the disconnects between the cultural norms you have and those your organization needs. Identify where your current talent investments are being undermined by the culture, and decide what to do about it.

6. **Evaluate whether you are doing everything you can to accelerate leadership development.** Leadership development is critical in most organizations today, and you can use the framework in Chapter 7 to see if you are missing opportunities in this area.

7. **Do whatever it takes to create and sustain urgency around solving your most critical talent problems.** This may mean using new measures or confronting your staff with troubling data from outside the organization, as described in Chapter 9. Once your objectives are clear, no executive action is more important than motivating productive action on workforce and leadership issues. Sustaining this urgency over time will be one of your greatest challenges.

Is a Talent Shortage the Next Predictable Surprise?

Despite the distractions of increased unemployment in recent years, the talent and leadership crises facing most organizations in the years ahead are very real. In the last decade we have seen governance failures that resulted first from accounting and financial malpractices that produced the failures of Enron, Worldcom, and so on. More recently, the world plunged into a recession when corporate leadership encouraged excessive risk-taking in overheated financial markets.[10]

The question is, Will the next round of governance failures be driven by inadequate attention to talent management? Will executive teams and their boards fail to manage the evolving risks created by the shortages of leadership and skilled professionals needed to sustain and grow today's complex organizations? We hope not. But, as the saying goes, "Hope is not a method."[11] As a leader, the method and mind-set you need starts with the tools and frameworks we have provided here. Good luck!

Appendix

A Checklist for the Effective Executive

Questions That Make a Difference
in Managing Talent

As we said in Chapter 1, the career experience that led you to your current position probably did not include a stint on a talent management staff, yet you still must be a strong leader on talent issues. You can create an environment where the highest priority talent management efforts get the attention and resources they need by asking thoughtful questions, not only in conversations that specifically focus on talent problems, but also in conversations that address general business priorities, risks, and opportunities.

Use the following questions to make these discussions and reviews as productive as possible. For more details in answering these questions, see the chapters noted in parentheses.

Create Awareness

Demonstrate your belief in the importance of broad-based talent management (Chapters 1, 3).

- Do we have a talent management strategy? What is it? What are we choosing to do and choosing *not* to do that reflect our strategy?
- How is our talent management strategy helping us build the workforce and leadership team we need to drive the business in the future?
- In any conversation about a transition (e.g., adding a product, adding a market, adding a geographical location, acquiring a company, divesting a company, reorganizing the business), what are the talent implications of the change?

Define Your Role
Let colleagues know what to expect from you (Chapters 1, 2, 8, 9).

- What do you need from me, as the leader, when it comes to talent management?
- What are the talent management tasks I can't delegate?
- Which talent management activities are the highest priority and deserve my attention the most?
- Given limited time, how can I maximize my impact in shaping the organization's talent processes?
- How do I know I am doing my job well when it comes to managing talent?

Connect to Strategy
In talent management discussions, bring the focus back to strategy by ensuring that everyone in talent management can answer the "big picture" questions (Chapters 3, 4).

- Who are the customers or customer segments we serve, listed in priority order?
- What are the products or services we provide now, and which ones, if any, need to change as we implement the current strategy?
- With whom (and in what priority) do we partner in delivering our products or services?
- Who are our competitors (listed in priority order), why is each considered a threat, and what can we learn from them?
- How do we measure our success now, and how might that change in the future?
- What is the relevant history that affects our current business strategy?
- Which environmental trends or issues (such as market, economic, societal, political, or environmental factors) are important to our strategy?
- How does our organizational structure support our business strategy?
- What are three things our unit is doing to support the strategy?
- What are the leadership behaviors that we expect to be essential to our organization in the future? Are these behaviors aligned to support our strategy?
- Given our future strategy, what critical capabilities are most at risk in our organization?

Identify Risks

Determine which talent-related risks and problems are most critical (Chapter 4).

- What roles in our organization will be most difficult to fill, given competition in the market for talent, our geographic location, and the time it takes to develop adequate skills?
- How would a change in the availability or quality of talent have the greatest impact on the success of our organization?
- Specifically, what essential knowledge and capabilities are at risk? How do we track our critical silos of knowledge and the potential costs to the business if those capabilities are seriously disrupted?
- What assumptions are we making about the availability of critical talent in the marketplace, given our strategic objectives and the anticipated changes in our workforce and leadership team? How have we tested these assumptions?
- Whom are we competing with for critical new hires? What keeps good candidates from accepting our job offers?
- What are the risks to our leadership pipeline relative to our organization's growth plans? What are we doing to mitigate these risks?
- Describe the succession plan for all our C-level executives. Which leaders are participating? Who are the identified candidates for all strategically critical roles? How and how often are you validating the quality of the list?
- Which hard-to-fill leadership roles most often experience midcareer turnover?
- How are we developing and retaining managers capable of leading geographically distributed and culturally diverse teams in the future? How are we measuring our progress in this area?

- How do we know our onboarding processes adequately reduce the time it takes a new employee to get up to speed?
- How do we know that our compensation and benefits packages support our retention needs?
- What are the actual turnover rates for all critical roles or job families in our organization? Are these turnover rates trending in the right direction?
- What assumptions are we making about how changes in the economy, retirement eligibility, an improving stock market, and increased employment opportunities will affect unplanned attrition in key parts of our business?
- How do we know that our performance management process is robust enough to provide effective evaluations of all leaders?

Choose Talent Management Solutions

For both proposed initiatives and existing solutions, focus on business results (Chapters 5, 6, 7).

- How is this talent investment going to make us more effective? Is it net income, ROE, more favorable customer satisfaction surveys?
- Does this talent management program directly map to the business strategy, solving for an explicit need?
- Who is targeted with the program (e.g., new hires, a specific job function, or a specific team)?
- Who is the internal customer for the program (e.g., an executive sponsor or a specific line manager)?
- Who paid for the program (if it had direct costs), or who would have paid for it (if it did not have direct costs but used internal resources)?

- What is the timing?
- What does it cost (employee time plus external help)?
- How are the results tracked or measured?
- What is the history of this effort? If it failed in the past, why?
- What else is going on that is either parallel to or in conflict with this solution?
- What alternatives were considered?
- What are or would be the consequences of doing nothing?
- How does this talent management effort map to the business strategy and the cultural norms?
- Is there an exit strategy for this program, or will it go on indefinitely?
- What are the risks that the effort could fail (such as competing priorities), and what is being done to mitigate those risks?
- Who is developing the program, and what qualifies him or her to do a good job?
- How will you choose participants for the program?
- How will you follow the progress of the participants, and what are your contingency plans for people who don't do well in the program?
- What is the plan for long-term maintenance of the program?

Special Considerations for Technology Investments

When it comes to IT, focus on implementation, integration, and alignment with business objectives (Chapters 6, 9).

- How does this technology investment fit into our over-all talent management strategy? Is this system going to promote long-term integration—or unification—of talent processes? Or is it worth supporting as a stand-alone system because the benefits are so great?
- How will the outputs or benefits of this system support our business objectives? Will this system help us run the business better or identify and address talent-related threats to performance? Or is this system primarily for compliance purposes?
- What are we doing about the behavioral or cultural changes that will be required if managers and employees are to use these applications effectively?
- How will this system integrate with our legacy human resource information systems, enterprise systems, or existing talent applications? Is the CIO on board with this investment?
- How many executive sponsors have we talked to at existing customers for the vendors we are considering? How do their objectives and organizational context compare to ours?
- Are we trying to integrate talent management technology with old behaviors? Or are we also investing in creating new behaviors to maximize the capabilities of the new system? What is the plan for changing behaviors to effectively use the new technology?

Evaluate Existing Investments

For existing programs, look for improvements in productivity, consistency, and quality (Chapter 5).

- Which talent management programs or processes are most important for delivering on our business strategy?
- Which programs or processes are redundant?
- Which need additional resources?
- Which need stronger political support or sponsorship?
- Which programs should be cancelled or cut?
- Which could be consolidated or redesigned to increase quality and efficiency?
- Which need to be carefully (or more carefully) monitored? Which require little supervision?
- Which ones are so strong that they should be presented at an executive staff meeting or shared with colleagues in other divisions?

Measurement and Evaluation

Determine where measures will add the greatest value in decision making (Chapter 8).

- How are our measures of talent investments showing an impact on business outcomes?
- What talent-related decisions pose the greatest uncertainty and the greatest potential costs if we are wrong? What information would increase our chances of making the right decision? In other words, how can we reduce the uncertainty around the outcomes of this decision?
- What management decisions are these measurements supposed to support?
- How have we defined specifically what we want to achieve with this investment? What meaningful changes will be observable or detectable?

- If we can't detect meaningful changes after implementing this talent program, why are we still investing in it?
- How are we going to follow up to make sure the implications of measurements are understood and acted on?

Implementing Talent Initiatives

Create urgency, drive integration, and clarify sponsor's roles (Chapter 9).

- What behaviors have to change in the organization if this talent initiative is to be successful?
- What are we doing to connect key stakeholders with vivid data about the realities both outside and inside the organization that create a compelling need for change?
- Which talent outcomes will foster the greatest sense of urgency?
- What behaviors do our leaders need to promote urgency in the organization, and are we encouraging them whenever we can?
- How do we confront "urgency killers" directly, instead of just ignoring them?
- Have I met with colleagues to clarify who will play which specific roles in the implementation process? Have we clarified who has responsibility for key tasks?
- How do we examine existing and proposed talent programs from the employees' or users' perspective, focusing particularly on the handoffs between different stages in the employee life cycle?
- Have we asked our HR staff for ideas on how to smooth out problematic transitions or connections between stages in the talent life cycle?

- Do we have an updated inventory of existing and proposed talent management initiatives? Have I made my priorities clear to our staff? Have we addressed any sequencing issues?
- What steps are being taken to ensure talent management silos, like recruiting and management development, are better coordinated or integrated?

Questions Other Leaders Are Asking

To stay on the leading edge of talent management, consider the following questions (Chapter 10).

- Who "owns" talent management in our organization?
- What are we doing to ensure that line leaders in this company don't abdicate responsibility for talent management?
- How do we evaluate the talent management IQ of our executive team? When it comes to developing people, which of our executives are innovators, champions, conformers, or laggards?
- Are we promoting "laggards" into leadership roles where talent development is essential to organizational performance?
- If asked, how would our senior executive team show an accurate understanding of where all the high-potential talent is located in our organization?
- What are we doing to prevent line managers from hoarding high-potential talent?
- In what ways does our leadership team treat high-potential talent as a true organization-wide resource?
- How do we encourage our managers to focus on developing and retaining high potentials in key roles?

- What's my success rate in hiring my direct reports? How long does it usually take me to recognize a mistake in hiring? How long does it take me to deal with my mistakes?
- How do we hold our managers accountable for ignoring poor performance?
- Is our board of directors holding the chief executive accountable for effective C-level succession planning? Is the board playing an appropriate oversight role in the organization's talent management strategy?

Notes

Introduction

1. Claudio Fernández-Aráoz, "The Coming Fight for Executive Talent," *BusinessWeek*, December 7, 2009, 72.
2. See Edward E. Gordon, *Winning the Global Talent Showdown* (San Francisco: Berrett-Koehler, 2009); Tamara Erickson, *Plugged In: The Generation Y Guide to Thriving at Work* (Boston: Harvard Business School Press, 2008); Jennifer J. Deal, *Retiring the Generation Gap: How Employees Young and Old Can Find Common Ground* (San Francisco: Jossey-Bass, 2007); Ken Dychtwald, Tamara J. Erickson, and Robert Morison, *Workforce Crisis: How to Beat the Coming Shortage of Skills and Talent* (Boston: Harvard Business School Press, 2006); David W. DeLong, *Lost Knowledge: Confronting the Threat of an Aging Workforce* (New York: Oxford University Press, 2004); Lynne C. Lancaster and David Stillman, *When Generations Collide* (New York, Harper Business, 2002).
3. Susan M. Cantrell and David Smith, *Workforce of One: Revolutionizing Talent Management Through Customization* (Boston: Harvard Business School Press, 2010); Jac Fitz-Enz, *The New HR Analytics* (New York: AMACOM, 2010); Brian A. Becker, Mark A. Huselid, and Richard W. Beatty, *The Differentiated Workforce: Transforming Talent into Strategic Impact* (Boston: Harvard Business School Press, 2009); Dave Ulrich et al., *HR Transformation: Building Human Resources from*

the Outside In (New York: McGraw-Hill, 2009); Edward E. Lawler, *Talent: Making People Your Competitive Advantage* (San Francisco: Jossey-Bass, 2008); John W. Boudreau and Peter M. Ramstad, *Beyond HR: The New Science of Human Capital* (Boston: Harvard Business School Press, 2007).

Chapter 1

1. Deloitte Touche Tomatsu and the *Economist* Intelligence Unit, "Aligned at the Top," 2007.
2. Hewitt Associates and the Human Capital Institute, "The State of Talent Management," Talent Practices Impact Survey, October 2008; M. Guthridge et al., "Making Talent a Strategic Priority," *McKinsey Quarterly*, January 2008; M. Guthridge et al., "The People Problem in Talent Management," *McKinsey Quarterly*, no. 2, 2006; L. Morton, "Integrated and Integrative Talent Management: A Strategic Human Resource Framework," The Conference Board, Research Report 1345-04-RR; Fernández-Aráoz, "The Coming Fight for Executive Talent."
3. For a detailed discussion on the strategic impacts of changing workforce demographics and the costs of lost technical, scientific, and managerial knowledge, see DeLong, *Lost Knowledge.*
4. Hewitt, "The State of Talent Management"; Guthridge, "Making Talent a Strategic Priority"; C. McCauley, "Identify: A New View of Leading in a Diverse World," Online survey conducted by Center for Creative Leadership, *Leading Effectively* e-newsletter, July 2005; L. Gratton and C. Truss, "Three-Dimensional People Strategy: Putting Human Resources Policies into Action," *Academy of Management Executive* 17, no. 3 (2003).
5. Hewitt, "The State of Talent Management."
6. John Gillespie and David Zweig, *Money for Nothing: How the Failure of Corporate Boards Is Ruining American Business and Costing Us Trillions* (New York: Free Press, 2010); William D. Cohan, "Merrill Lynch's $50 Billion Feud," *Fortune*, April 15, 2010, http://money.cnn.com/2010/04/15/news/companies/merrill_lynch.fortune (accessed August 17, 2010).

7. David Larcker and Stephen A. Miles, "2010 Survey on CEO Succession Planning," Heidrick & Struggles and Rock Center for Corporate Governance, Stanford University Report, 2010, http://rockcenter.stanford.edu/wp-content/uploads/2010/06/CEO-Survey-Brochure-Final2.pdf (accessed October 26, 2010).

8. J. Nocera, "Incompetent? No, Just Not a Leader," *The New York Times*, October 3, 2009.

9. Michelle V. Rafter, "Shareholders Demand Better Window into CEO Succession," *Workforce Management*, June 2010.

10. Our thinking about risk management in this section is adapted from Peter Cappelli's *Talent on Demand: Managing Talent in an Age of Uncertainty* (Boston, MA: Harvard University Press, 2008).

11. Mary B. Young, "Implementing Strategic Workforce Planning," The Conference Board, Research Working Group Report 1444-09-RR, 2009.

12. B. Foss, "BP Audit: Key Job Vacant Before the Spill," *Washington Post*, September 8, 2006, http://www.washingtonpost.com/wp-dyn/content/article/2006/09/08/AR2006090800864_pf.html (accessed October 22, 2009).

13. Among the most notable are Cantrell and Smith, *Workforce of One*; Larry Israelite, ed., *Talent Management: Best Practices and Strategies for Success from Six Leading Companies* (New York: ASTD Press, 2010); Ulrich et al., *HR Transformation*; P. Cappelli, *Talent on Demand*; D. Ulrich and N. Smallwood, *Why the Bottom Line Isn't! How to Build Value Through People and Organization* (New York: Wiley, 2003); Becker, Huselid, and Beatty, *The Differentiated Workforce*; Lawler, *Talent*; M. Huselid et al., *The Workforce Scorecard* (Boston: HBS Press, 2005); and Boudreau and Ramstad, *Beyond HR*.

14. G. Becker, *Human Capital* (New York: Columbia University Press, 1964).

15. R. E. Ployhart et al., "The Structure and Function of Human Capital Emergence," *Academy of Management Journal* 40, no. 4 (2006): 661.

16. Young, "Implementing Strategic Workforce Planning."

17. For an excellent discussion of differing definitions of *talent management*, see Israelite, *Talent Management.*
18. Young, "Implementing Strategic Workforce Planning."
19. Constance E. Helfat et al., "The Pipeline to the Top: Women and Men in the Top Executive Ranks of U.S. Corporations," *Academy of Management Perspectives*, 2004.

Chapter 2
1. Diana Brady, "Can GE Still Manage?" *BusinessWeek*, April 25, 2010, 27–32.

Chapter 3
1. Jeffrey E. Garteen, *The Mind of the CEO* (New York: Basic Books, 2001), 149.
2. Of course, realigning—or changing—organizational structures, systems, or cultures may also be necessary to implement business strategy, but these issues have been dealt with by many authors and are more widely accepted as top management responsibilities. For example, see Michael Watkins, *The First 90 Days* (Boston: Harvard Business School Press, 2003).
3. These barriers to strategic alignment are adapted from Christopher Meyer's analysis in *Fast Cycle Time: How to Align Purpose, Strategy, and Structure for Speed* (New York: The Free Press, 1993).
4. Meyer, *Fast Cycle Time.*
5. B. Groysberg and E. Sherman, "Baker & McKenzie (A): A New Framework for Talent Management," Case Study 9-408-009 (Boston, MA: Harvard Business School Publishing, 2008).

Chapter 4
1. Douglas W. Hubbard, *The Failure of Risk Management* (New York: Wiley, 2010); David Ropeik, *How Risky Is It Really? Why Our Fears Don't Always Match the Facts* (New York: McGraw-Hill, 2010).
2. Of course, risk also implies the possibility of a positive outcome, which is what entrepreneurs bet on all the time. But in

terms of talent, given current changes in the workforce, most leaders are primarily concerned with avoiding the negative outcomes posed by risks.

3. Groysberg and Sherman, "Baker & McKenzie (A)."
4. For a more detailed discussion of identifying and prioritizing these risks, see Becker, Huselid, and Beatty, *The Differentiated Workforce.*
5. Hubbard, *The Failure of Risk Management*, 17.
6. Ibid., 45.
7. K. Buehler et al., "The Risk Revolution: The New Arsenal of Risk Management," *Harvard Business Review*, September 2008.
8. These domains are well described by Hubbard in *The Failure of Risk Management.* For a more general story of the rise of the "quant school" of risk management, see Peter L. Bernstein, *Against the Gods: The Remarkable Story of Risk* (New York: Wiley, 1996); Benoit Mandelbrot and Richard L. Hudson, *The (Mis)Behavior of Markets* (New York: Basic Books, 2004); and Michael T. Carpenter, *The Risk-Wise Investor: How to Better Understand and Manage Risk* (New York: Wiley, 2009).
9. Hubbard, *The Failure of Risk Management.*
10. Ibid.
11. Douglas Hubbard and Douglas A. Samuelson, "Analysis Placebos," *Analytics Magazine*, Fall 2009.
12. For a detailed description of how to apply quantitative risk management tools to more qualitative problems like talent management, see Hubbard, *The Failure of Risk Management.*
13. Christoph H. Loch et al., "How BMW Is Defusing the Demographic Time Bomb," *Harvard Business Review*, March 2010; Rainer Strack, Jens Baier, and Anders Fahlander, "Managing Demographic Risk," *Harvard Business Review*, February 2008.
14. For details on Rodgers' process, see L. Branham, "Should You Try to Win Back Top Performers When They Resign? One Company's Success Story," *Keeping the People Report 6*, 2005 holiday issue, http://www.keepingthepeople.com/newsletter/vol-06-holiday-2005.html (accessed August 2, 2010).

15. Ibid.
16. DeLong, *Lost Knowledge.*

Chapter 5
1. Edgar H. Schein, *The Corporate Culture Survival Guide* (San Francisco: Jossey-Bass, 1999).
2. See Schein, *The Corporate Culture Survival Guide,* for a practical guide to diagnosing culture. Also see David W. DeLong and Liam Fahey, "Diagnosing Cultural Barriers to Knowledge Management," *Academy of Management Executive* 14, no. 4 (2000).

Chapter 6
1. "Electronic Arts Embraces Social Networking to Create Better Games on Tight Timelines," Microsoft Office Systems Customer Solutions Case Study, May 2009, http://tinyurl .com/24s27sy (accessed May 18, 2010).
2. This case is adapted from "Westpac Banking Corporation Delivers Workforce of the Future with Careers@Westpac," Taleo Case Study, 2007, http://www.taleo.com/casestudy/ westpac-banking-corporation-delivers-workforce-future-ca reerswestpac (accessed July 1, 2010).
3. David DeLong, "Case Study: Fanning the Flame to Retain Boomer Nurses," MetLife MatureMarket Institute, 2009, http://whymetlife.com/downloads/MetLife_MMI_MultiGen-CaseStudies.pdf (accessed September 28, 2010).
4. Study cited in William B. P. Robson, "Aging Populations and the Workplace," British-North American Research Association Statement 20, October 2001, http://www.cdhowe.org/pdf/ BNAC_Aging_Populations.pdf (accessed July 1, 2010).
5. For more details on the Aerospace Corporation's Retiree Casual Program, see David DeLong and Associates, "Searching for the Silver Bullet: Leading Edge Solutions for Leveraging an Aging Workforce," MetLife Mature Market Institute Study, November 2007.

Chapter 7

1. Ray B. Williams, "CEO Failures: How On-Boarding Can Help," *Psychology Today*, May 2, 2010, http://tinyurl .com/33rwlku (accessed May 26, 2010); Nat Stoddard and Claire Wyckoff, "The Costs of CEO Failure," *Chief Executive*, November/December 2008; Jena McGregor, "How to Take the Reins at Top Speed," *BusinessWeek*, February 5, 2007, http:// www.businessweek.com/magazine/content/07_06/b4020077 .htm (accessed May 26, 2010).
2. Williams, "CEO Failures."
3. Carlotta Vollhardt, "Pfizer's Prescription for the Risky Business of Executive Transitions," *Journal of Organizational Excellence*, Winter 2005.
4. For a detailed description of the contents of the Peer Mentoring workshop, see Steve Trautman, *Teach What You Know: A Practical Leaders Guide to Knowledge Transfer* (Upper Saddle River, NJ: Prentice-Hall, 2007).
5. The RASCI model is a tool used to identify roles and responsibilities during an organizational change initiative. See Chapter 9 for a detailed illustration.
6. For a detailed description of how to create skill development plans, see Trautman, *Teach What You Know: A Practical Leader's Guide to Knowledge Transfer Using Peer Mentoring*.
7. For a detailed discussion on the strategic impacts of changing workforce demographics, see DeLong, *Lost Knowledge*.
8. Jean Martin and Conrad Schmidt, "How to Keep Your Top Talent," *Harvard Business Review*, May 2010, 54–61.
9. Diane Brady, "Can GE Still Manage?" *Bloomberg BusinessWeek*, April 25, 2010, 31–32.
10. Martin and Schmidt, "How to Keep Your Top Talent."
11. Ibid.
12. Ibid.

Chapter 8

1. Douglas W. Hubbard, *How to Measure Anything: Finding the Value of Intangibles in Business* (Hoboken, NJ: John Wiley and Sons, 2007); Boudreau and Ramstad, *Beyond HR*.

2. The topic of measurement is broad and multifaceted. Thus, a thorough description of the measurement processes relevant to talent management is beyond the scope of a single chapter. For a detailed description of a talent-related measurement process, see Boudreau and Ramstad, *Beyond HR*; Wayne Cascio and John Boudreau, *Investing in People: Financial Impact of Human Resource Initiatives* (Upper Saddle River, NJ: FT Press, 2008), 7–8.

3. Boudreau and Ramstad, *Beyond HR*, 208.

4. Boudreau and Ramstad, *Beyond HR*, 190.

5. Hubbard, *How to Measure Anything*, 47.

6. Cascio and Boudreau, *Investing in People*, 7–8.

7. Jonathan Low and Pam Cohen Kalafut, *Invisible Advantages: How Intangibles Are Driving Business Performance* (Cambridge, MA: Perseus Publishing, 2002); Jonathan Low and Tony Siesfeld, "Measures That Matter: Wall Street Considers Non-Financial Performance More than You Think," *Strategy and Leadership* 26, no. 2 (Mar–Apr 1998): 24–31.

8. Hubbard, *How to Measure Anything*.

9. This section is derived primarily from Douglas Hubbard's excellent treatise on measuring intangibles, *How to Measure Anything*.

10. Hubbard, *How to Measure Anything*, 83.

11. Boudreau and Ramstad, *Beyond HR*, 193–194.

12. Larcker and Miles, "2010 Survey on CEO Succession Planning," Heidrick & Struggles and Rock Center for Corporate Governance, Stanford University Report, 2010, http://www .gsb.stanford.edu/cldr/cgrp/documents/CEOSurveyBrochure Final.pdf. (accessed August 5, 2010).

13. Gillespie and Zweig, *Money for Nothing*; David F. Larcker and Brian Tayan, "CEO Succession Planning: Who's Behind Door Number One?" Stanford Graduate School of Business Research Note CGRP-05, June 24, 2010, http://www.gsb .stanford.edu/cldr/cgrp/documents/CGRP05-Succession.pdf (accessed August 16, 2010).

14. Jennifer Reingold, "CEO Swap: The $79 Billion Plan," *Fortune*, November 19, 2009, http://www.mutualfundsmag

.us/2009/11/19/news/companies/procter_gamble_lafley.for
tune/index.htm (accessed August 16, 2010).

15. Cascio and Boudreau, *Investing in People*, 195.

16. Ibid.

17. R. Strack, J. Baier, and A. Fahlander, "Managing Demographic Risk," *Harvard Business Review*, February 2008, 123.

18. Our ideas about the relationship between measurement and decisions are adapted from Hubbard, *How to Measure Anything*.

19. Hubbard, *How to Measure Anything*, 43.

20. Hubbard, *How to Measure Anything*; another good source on this topic is Martin, Roger, "Why Good Spreadsheets Make Bad Strategies," Harvard Business Review Blog, January 11, 2010, http://blogs.hbr.org/martin/2010/01/why-good-spread sheets-make-bad.html (accessed August 5, 2010).

21. Jean Martin and Conrad Schmidt, "How to Keep Your Top Talent," *Harvard Business Review*, May 2010, 54–61.

22. Boudreau and Ramstad, *Beyond HR*; Fitz-Enz, *The New HR Analytics*.

23. Ulrich and Smallwood, *Why the Bottom Line Isn't!*

24. Grae Yohe, "The Talent Solution," *Human Resource Executive OnLine*, June 2, 2009, http://www.hreonline.com/HRE/story .jsp?storyId=215102562&query=The%20Talent%20Solution (accessed August 7, 2010).

25. Boudreau and Ramstad, *Beyond HR*.

26. John P. Kotter and Dan S. Cohen, *The Heart of Change: Real-Life Stories of How People Change Their Organizations* (Boston: Harvard Business School Press, 2002).

Chapter 9

1. John P. Kotter, *A Sense of Urgency* (Boston: Harvard Business School Press, 2008), viii.

2. See, for example, Hans Henrick Jørgensen, Lawrence Owen, and Andreas Neus, "Making Change Work," an IBM study, 2008, http://www-935.ibm.com/services/us/gbs/bus/html/gbs-making-change-work.html; Marc Vinson, Caroline Pung, and Javier Muñiz Gonzáles-Blanch, "Organizing for Successful

Change Management: A McKinsey Global Survey," *McKinsey Quarterly*, June 2006.

3. Some excellent books for leaders on managing change include John P. Kotter, *Leading Change* (Boston: Harvard Business School Press, 1996); Robert E. Quinn, *Deep Change: Discovering the Leader Within* (San Francisco: Jossey-Bass, 1996); *Harvard Business Review on Change* (Boston: Harvard Business School Press, 1998); Dave Ulrich et al., eds., *The Change Champion's Field Guide: Strategies and Tools for Leading Change in Your Organization* (New York: Best Practice Publications, 2003); and Chip Heath and Dan Heath, *Switch: How to Change Things When Change Is Hard* (New York: Broadway Books, 2010).

4. Kotter, *A Sense of Urgency*, 13.

5. For a detailed discussion of complacency and false urgency and potential solutions, see Kotter, *A Sense of Urgency*.

6. Dan Ciampa, "No Sense of Urgency," *The Conference Board Review*, April 2009.

7. John Kotter and Holger Rathgeber, *Our Iceberg Is Melting: Changing and Succeeding Under Any Conditions* (New York: St. Martins Press, 2005); Kotter, *A Sense of Urgency*.

8. For more on coalition building see Kotter, *Leading Change*; Larry Hirschhorn, "Campaigning for Change," *Harvard Business Review*, July 2002.

9. H. Kerzner, *Project Management: A Systems Approach to Planning, Scheduling, and Controlling* (Hoboken, NJ: John Wiley and Sons, 2006).

10. Josh Bersin, "The Business of Talent Management," in Israelite, *Talent Management*.

11. Nigel Paine, "Talent Management: The Elephant in the Room," in Israelite, *Talent Management*.

Chapter 10

1. Annmarie Neal and Robert Kovach, "Talent Management: Function and Transformation at Cisco—the Demands of the Global Economy," in Israelite, *Talent Management*.

2. The most thorough case made for this approach is Becker, Huselid, and Beatty, *The Differentiated Workforce*.

3. Alan Weiss and Nancy MacKay, *The Talent Advantage: How to Attract and Retain the Best and the Brightest* (Hoboken, NJ: John Wiley and Sons, 2009).

4. William Pasmore, "Who Will Run Your Company? Aligning Leadership Development with Long-Term Strategy," *The Conference Board Review*, Summer 2010, 23–26.

5. For a useful summary of what makes performance management processes really work and ideas for increasing accountability, see Marc Effron and Miriam Ort, *One Page Talent Management* (Boston: Harvard Business School Press, 2010).

6. Jennifer Reingold, "CEO Swap: The $79 Billion Plan."

7. Gillespie and Zweig, *Money for Nothing*.

8. For details on this classic management dilemma, see Steven Kerr's article, "On the Folly of Rewarding A, While Hoping for B," *Academy of Management Executive*, 9, no. 1 (1995).

9. Chip Heath and Dan Heath, *Made to Stick: Why Some Ideas Survive and Others Die* (New York: Random House, 2007).

10. Gillespie and Zweig, *Money for Nothing*.

11. Gordon R. Sullivan and Michael V. Harper, *Hope Is Not a Method: What Business Leaders Can Learn from America's Army* (New York: Broadway Books, 1997).

Index

Note: Page numbers followed by *f* or *t* refer to figures or tables respectively.